T0162672

THE VOID WITHIN

An Inner Quest for Wholeness

ARNOLD C. HARMS, PH.D.

THE VOID WITHIN
An Inner Quest for Wholeness

iUniverse books may be ordered through booksellers or by contacting:

iUniverse
1663 Liberty Drive
Bloomington, IN 47403
www.iuniverse.com
1-800-Authors (1-800-288-4677)

Because of the dynamic nature of the Internet, any web addresses or
links contained in this book may have changed since publication and
may no longer be valid. The views expressed in this work are solely those
of the author and do not necessarily reflect the views of the publisher,
and the publisher hereby disclaims any responsibility for them.

Any people depicted in stock imagery provided by Thinkstock are models,
and such images are being used for illustrative purposes only.
Certain stock imagery © Thinkstock.

ISBN: 978-1-4917-3152-9 (sc)
ISBN: 978-1-4917-3153-6 (e)

Print information available on the last page.

iUniverse rev. date: 04/06/2015

CONTENTS

PREFACE

A preface properly concerns those things that the reader needs to know prior to engaging the text. It should frame the inquiry by indicating: (1) the scope of the investigation; (2) what is presupposed by the inquiry; (3) the methodology to be used; and (4) what it intends to accomplish.

Any adequate discussion of the *void within* requires that one provide both its philosophical justification and its location within the broader context of humanistic studies. Inevitably, that involves one in a plethora of technical terms drawn from the various fields of study: philosophy, psychology, literature, etc. However, since this work was written for lay persons, professional jargon is held to a minimum; terms that prove unavoidable are explained within the text. For readers who still find these prefatory remarks tedious, it is recommended that they skip the Preface and go directly to Chapter One perhaps, returning to the Preface at a later time.

First, concerning the scope of the investigation, the title, The Void Within: An Inner Quest for Wholeness, rightly suggests that this is an inquiry into self-understanding. It probes the universal, human experience that something seems to be missing within the human psyche—something vital that cries out for explanation and resolution. What is the nature of the void within the human soul, and what does that inner void represent? Any attempt to answer those provocative questions soon involves one in the larger questions of what constitutes a self; and what are the structures of selfhood?

This naturally leads the inquiry to an examination of what is meant by an authentic and/or inauthentic self. Finally, one must ask: what is required to "fill the void" within the human heart, bringing one a sense of fulfillment and satisfaction?

An exposition of the inner void eventually faces one with the grounding question of all philosophy and psychology: What does it mean to be human? One will readily note that what began as a very limited, introspective analysis, quickly became the broadest possible question for humanistic studies. Understanding what it means to be human also involves the question about how human reality is to be interpreted vis-à-vis its place on the infinite cosmic stage upon which modern humans find themselves.

The expansion on our initial question reminds one of the comment made by Joseph Campbell regarding Sigmund Freud's discovery of the unconscious mind: "He was fishing while sitting on the back of a whale." Freud had not yet fully realized the magnitude of what he had uncovered. It was left to those who followed, like Carl Jung, to elucidate the full scope of the collective unconscious and its role in producing dreams, symbols, archetypal patterns, mythology, religious language, etc. Likewise, that which began for us as a limited and narrowly defined problem of the self, quickly became an inquiry without limits—as broad and comprehensive as human reality itself.

Second, every inquiry begins with certain presuppositions. There is no presuppositionless inquiry. Without first supposing something to be true, questions would not arise. It is only when experience contradicts that which is assumed to be true, does one ask, Why? It is this unique power to question that enables the human to be defined as the Inquiring Animal. A fuller description of this awesome mental power is detailed in the chapter on The Grandeur of Man.

Presupposed in this study is the reality and primacy of the self in the context of the world. The self-world combination is essential because consciousness is always consciousness of something. Consciousness intends, or points to, some entity within its world. This study eschews all idealistic assumptions that would understand the world as a projection of the self.

It also assumes the Cartesian <u>Cogito</u> as its starting point. The seventeenth century philosopher, Rene Descartes, who is considered to be the father of modern philosophy, sought absolute certainty for his philosophy. In order to locate a bedrock starting point upon which to ground his philosophy, Descartes began with methodological doubt—doubting everything until he could find that which was indubitable. He soon discovered that he could doubt everything—except one thing—he could not doubt the fact that he was doubting. In order to doubt, he had to think, and by thinking, he knew that he existed. Thus the classic expression of the <u>Cogito</u>, "I think, therefore, I am." Descartes had found his indubitable starting point.

The import of this methodological beginning is that it locates its primary certainty within the human situation and not in some external metaphysical, theological or philosophical system. Epistemologically, this amounted to a Copernican Revolution in philosophy. The human self from then on would be central rather than peripheral to any understanding of existence.

Some have criticized the argument of the <u>Cogito</u>, saying that it is too intellectualistic. They say that it was formulated by someone who greatly underestimated the impact of a toothache. One is reminded of a line from a poem by Claribel Algeria, "I hurt, therefore I exist."[1] Indeed, we know that we exist because of pain. We are feeling, willing, caring beings,

---

[1]   A line from the poem, "I am a mirror" by Claribel Algeria, found in <u>The Bedford Introduction to Learning</u>, ed., Michael Meyer, (Boston: Bedford's Books of St. Martin's Press, 1990), pp. 877-878.

not just rational minds. This knowledge is intuited by the self. It is direct, unmediated, personal and self-evident. It is available to everyone through self-reflection; although, one need not reflect on it to experience its reality. But these arguments do not refute Descartes; they only confirm and expand upon his position.

After having secured his indubitable starting point, Descartes focused on the next logical question: I am; but <u>what</u> am I? Descartes responded to that query with an affirmation that man is a "thinking thing," <u>res cogitans</u>. That definition of man, according to the existentialist philosopher Jean-Paul Sartre, was Descartes' fatal mistake. By using the impersonal language of thinghood instead of the vocabulary of personhood to refer to human reality, he set philosophy on the wrong course. According to Sartre, one must begin with consciousness. In order to say, "I am," one intuitively must be aware of one's existence; and to be self-aware is to instinctively know that one is a conscious being. Consciousness includes awareness. The exploration of what it means to be a conscious being leads to the next critical question of this inquiry: what is the proper methodology to be used to probe the <u>inner void</u>, and hence the inmost needs of the self?

Third, the methodology employed by this study is best described as <u>phenomenological existentialism</u>. This jawbreaker term points to the fact that any analysis of what it means to be human must begin within human existence itself. The term <u>existence</u> comes from two Latin words, <u>ex</u> and <u>sistere</u>, which means, "to stand out from." Human existence stands out from the rest of being through its self-transcending freedom. It is constantly re-creating itself through its free choices. Hence human existence is characterized by freedom.

If some learned, behaviorist professor were to write a twenty volume treatise on why humans were determined and had no freedom, it would be presented to the human community to judge whether its conclusions were valid. The irony of humans being asked to <u>decide</u> whether or not they were free apparently would have escaped the learned professor altogether. Freedom is intuited directly by the self. The self does not need three good reasons to know that it is free. Any methodology that would investigate what it means to be human must necessarily take this fact into account.

The scientific method was designed to examine empirical reality; and therefore, would be totally inappropriate to probe the inner workings of the human psyche because it is not an empirical reality. The scientific method can deal with randomness and uncertainty, but not freedom. That is a wholly different category. The psyche lies outside the realm of science. A methodology more appropriate to human reality is required.

That was the concern of the philosopher Edmund Husserl, who developed a method for analyzing phenomena that was not just empirical, but covered the whole range of experience that makes up human existence. Husserl sought to investigate the principles that govern various types of objects of consciousness. As Catherine Brosman notes, "Consciousness perceives, imagines, judges, intuits, values, constructs, and thus gives meaning to the world."[2] Husserl accepted the Kantian conclusion of 150 years earlier that the rational mind can know empirical reality only as it presents itself through sense impressions; therefore, it cannot know the thing-in-itself. The Kantian approach limited knowledge to that which can be empirically verified. Husserl sought a method whereby one might affirm a wider range of knowledge by analyzing <u>all</u> phenomena as it presents itself to human life. He called this new method <u>phenomenological analysis</u>.

The word "phenomenology" comes from the Greek word, <u>phainesthai</u>, which means "to appear." The self can have valid knowledge of that which appears to it as part of its

---

[2]   Catherine Savage Brossman, <u>Jean-Paul Sartre</u>, (Boston, Massachusetts: G. K. Hannand and Co., 1983), p. 19.

world. This wider knowledge encompasses things like beauty, music, artistic expression, the psyche, logic, mathematics, etc.—things valued by the self, but are not scientifically or empirically verifiable. Nevertheless, Husserl said that these intangible values must be a part of legitimate knowledge. They are subject to direct experience by the existing self and therefore, have their own form of validation.

Husserl bracketed out all scientific assumptions that would treat the human being as a thing-among-things. He rejected any approach that would diminish the valid experience of human beings in their encounter with the phenomena of the world. Existentialists that followed in his wake, like Sartre, bracketed out all metaphysical, theological, philosophical and sociological systems that would interpret the self from a perspective outside of its self-world relationship. Sartre accepted Husserl's phenomenological approach for his philosophy of existentialism, omitting certain idealistic assumptions by Husserl such as the Transcendental Ego, which was supposed to guarantee the unity and reality of the self.[3] Sartre said that there was no need for that presupposition in order to understand the existing self as embedded in its world. One can proceed directly to an examination of the existing self and give an existential description of authentic and inauthentic modes of existence. Thus one can plumb the depths of the human psyche and arrive at knowledge of what it means to be fully human.

No grand metaphysical system is necessary to arrive at an understanding of authentic existence. The general approach and methodology outlined by Sartre is, likewise, adopted by this inquiry as it probes the <u>void in the human soul</u>.

---

[3]   Edmund Husserl postulated a Transcendental Ego to guarantee the unity of the phenomenal self. It was a concept like the Eternal Forms of Plato that were the true reality standing behind the changing flux of temporal existence.

Fourth, the intended goal of this inquiry is not only to analyze what is meant by the inner void; it is also aimed at uncovering what it takes to fill that void and bring happiness and a sense of fulfillment to the existing self. In such a phenomenological analysis of the self and its needs, our inquiry looks to that which brings completeness and wholeness to the self. Finding that "missing something" is the goal of the inner quest into what it means to be fully human. Filling the inner void, and hence living an authentic existence, is what this study refers to as living the Beautiful Life.

This inquiry has been problem driven. Initially, its outcome was unknown—unlike certain formula-religion books that "know" the answer in advance and treat the problem only insofar as it ratifies their predetermined answer. This study began with no such predetermined answer in mind; rather, it left the outcome wide open. Moreover, the answers that this study did arrive at, though valid, are in no way exhaustive or final. They are provisional and tentative—suggestive of a more comprehensive humanistic answer that, ultimately, can only be provided by the concrete deeds and actions of the human race itself. What it means to be authentically human ultimately can only be determined by the human spirit as it creatively expresses itself through the projects and accomplishments of its own history.

There are many pitfalls and obstacles that must be encountered along the way; but if successful, the journey and prize that awaits at the conclusion of this odyssey of the soul will, I hope, be more than worth the effort.

Chapter I

UNDERSTANDING THE VOID

The concern of this study is the <u>void within the human soul</u>. Most people readily identify with that topic. It resonates with something deep within their inmost being. The problem addressed is immediately recognized as one that is their own. It is the universal experience that something is missing in one's life—something vital and important for one's sense of wholeness as a human being. Yet the individual often cannot put a finger on exactly what is missing. There is a vague awareness that all is not right with the self. Consciousness of this problem might come and go depending upon the circumstances of life; but it is always there as a dark counterpoint to the melody of life. When put in those terms, many respond, "That, in a nutshell, is the story of my life."

For want of a better term, this inarticulate feeling that something is amiss we have called, the <u>inner void</u>. Accompanying the awareness of this void is an instinctive yearning that the need be met—but with what? What is it that the human psyche longs for and requires to make it feel whole and complete? What need must be met for the human being to achieve fulfillment and happiness? Finding the answer to that question is the holy grail of the soul's inner quest. In order to attain the goal of that quest, we must first examine the nature of the void: What is it? Why should it interest anyone? And finally, how is it encountered?

Regarding the first question, the problem of the void turns out to be two-pronged. The first prong involves the <u>outer physical void,</u> i.e., the void as encountered outside the human psyche.

An extended answer to what is meant by the <u>outer void</u> has been given in Chapter II on the Concept of the Void. However, for our present purpose, it suffices to say that the primary meaning of the term is the <u>absence of all matter</u>, or, <u>space without matter</u>.

The outer, or external void, constitutes the infinite cosmic stage upon which the human drama is played out. What is meant by that will become clear as the study progresses. Since the outer void was defined as nothingness, or space without matter, the problem becomes: how does one discuss nothing? Perhaps, nothing can be said about nothing; but something can be said about the human experience of nothingness, a.k.a., the void.

The experience of voidness is universal and pervasive, impacting every person. Consequently, a legitimate form of inquiry is to analyze and seek to understand humans as they encounter the void.

This leads to the second prong, which has to do with the <u>inner spiritual void</u>. In this case, the term <u>void</u> is used in a secondary metaphorical sense. It refers to the absence of everything required for a meaningful human existence. If the external spatial void was defined as "nothingness", "non-being", or "empty space", the second, or inner spiritual void, refers to the "emptiness", "hollowness", or "meaninglessness" experienced in one's inmost being. The first type is a component of the physical universe; whereas, the second refers to the depths of the human soul. The main focus of the study is on the second, or metaphorical, usage of the term; however, in order to understand the concept of the void in its full dimensions, it will be necessary to examine both the physical and metaphorical types.

Regarding the second question about why should the issue interest anyone, it is important because it plays a vital role in shaping human existence. Sooner or later, everyone will encounter the void and they must come to terms with it. How one responds to it can make all the difference between living an authentic or inauthentic existence. One can either flee from the void, or face it. If we fail to successfully come to terms with the void, then we forfeit the chance to become a whole person. We not only can ask, we <u>must</u> ask about the void, because failure to do so results in inauthenticity and the loss of full selfhood.

The void in the human heart means that something vital is absent. It has an ominous aspect to it in that it indicates that the individual has been deprived of that which is desired and required to live a full and happy life. It is an experience of emptiness or deprivation within the soul. The loss is not something trivial, but is of such magnitude as to be critical for the human being. The issue is deeply personal and concerns every human being, whether consciously or unconsciously. It constitutes an existential crisis for the individual.

Spinoza (1632-1677) once declared that "nature abhors a vacuum."[1] It seems that the void in nature <u>must</u> be filled. For example, a bolt of lightning is a discharge of atmospheric electricity that creates a vacuum. The accompanying thunderclap is the loud crash caused by the surrounding air rushing in to fill that vacuum. Likewise, nature's abhorrence of a vacuum is matched by the self's abhorrence of the inner void which <u>must be filled at all cost</u>.

Regarding the third question, one can encounter the void almost anywhere, but the most common way is in facing the possibility of one's own inevitable death. We are, as Eugene O'Neil's play suggests, all on that "Long Day's Journey into Night." Death is the end of existence as we know it. It is the

---

[1]   Benedict (Baruch) Spinoza, <u>Ethics</u>, pt. I, proposition 35; note.

ultimate nothingness for the human soul. People may tell themselves comforting stories and myths about personal existence beyond the grave, but this is based more on wishful thinking than hard evidence.

Consequently, humans universally have angst before the void. They instinctively feel uneasy and uncomfortable even at the mention of it. The very word seems to be a threat to all that is life-affirming. Why is that? The void represents the mysterious unknown, the irrational, chaotic and uncontrollable, i.e., all that is alien to human existence. As such, it is scary and anxiety-producing.

It should be pointed out here that there is a fundamental difference between <u>fear</u> and <u>anxiety</u>. Fear is directed toward a definite object or event; whereas, anxiety is not. One might have certain phobias such as acrophobia, the fear of heights. The person with an obsession disorder regarding height is often afraid to cross a bridge for fear of falling off. When riding a mule down the Grand Canyon, there are places where the trail follows along a narrow ledge and where the shear drop off is two or three thousand feel straight down from the trail. One misstep of the mule might plunge the rider into the abyss. Few people pass along these places without feeling a tinge of fear.

The grim reality of death is a good example of the difference between fear and anxiety. One might be fearful of a special form of death, e.g., drowning, so that the individual might panic at the thought of entering a body of water. One can be taught not to fear water by learning how to swim, or to take other defensive measures; but death, as such, causes universal anxiety and cannot be removed. It is the unnamable void that awaits everyone.

Anxiety, however, has no object toward which it is directed. If anything, anxiety is engendered by nothingness— by the indefinable threat of the void. It is like being alone and lost on the Great Saharan Dessert with nothing but hot burning sand dunes extending endlessly into the horizon in all directions. One is totally helpless and at the mercy of fate. Likewise, one is defenseless in the face of the void.

Psychiatry can cure phobias, but not angst before the void. It is the ineradicable part of human existence and cannot be removed by therapy. Each person must learn how to live and cope with it in his or her own way.

There are three principal sources of anxiety, according to the philosopher of religion Paul Tillich. Each has its relative and absolute form.[2]

1. Fate and Death
2. Guilt and Condemnation
3. Emptiness and Meaninglessness

Although each is different in its own concern, all three are but masks for the all-encompassing void. Death, as has been shown, is the loss of existence. It is being swallowed up by the infinite void. Next, moral condemnation carries with it the loss of one's future hope and destiny. And lastly, meaninglessness is a final surrender to the absurdity of the human predicament in face of the abysmal void.

Nothing makes one more aware of the inner void than a sense of emptiness and meaninglessness in the human heart. The problem has become especially acute in today's Postmodern World where there has been a total loss of any overarching framework of meaning. In the words of Richard Tarnas, the postmodern collapse of meaning has exposed a "yawning void of relativism left by modernity's dissolution of traditional world views."[3] As a consequence of this event in the intellectual history of the Western Mind, "the postmodern human exists in a universe whose significance is

---

[2] Paul Tillich, <u>The Courage to Be</u>, (New York: Yale University Press, 1952), pp. 40-51.

[3] Richard Tarnas, <u>The Passion of the Western Mind</u>, (New York: Ballantine Books, 1991), p. 412.

at once utterly open and without foundation."[4] According to Tarnas, inhabitants of the 21st century live in a world that has been totally relativized and without any meta-narrative by which society could be guided and bound together.

An example of this would be the loss of the framework of meaning once enjoyed by the human race in the Pre-Copernican Age. At that time, it was a finite, closed world in which most questions had ready answers. No one any longer accepts that view of a universe with its stationary earth located at the center. Today, every schoolchild knows that the earth orbits the sun, not vice versa.

The human being has undergone a radical displacement from a central to a relative and peripheral position in a vast and impersonal universe. This change in cosmology has had profound consequences for the self-image of humankind. The human is no longer a special divine creation in a cozy, closed world. Man is only one animal among millions of species that have evolved over billions of years. Mankind has no privileged place in the scheme of things and could become extinct like the dinosaurs. Everything about the human reality and its world has been relativized so that there are no longer any absolutes to cling to for security or to determine one's course of action.

In response to this radical change in cosmology, the 21st century person has been forced to re-think his/her image of mankind. Old images and forms no longer communicate to a rootless and relativized age faced with an absurd universe. This has produced a crisis in human self-understanding that has resulted in global anxiety and <u>ennui</u>.

Of course, there are those who, for one reason or another, refuse to come to terms with the Postmodern Age. They cling to past mythologies and outdated world views. They have been termed "flat-earth" people. They are those who refuse to rethink their first century ideas in light of the 21st century.

---

4   <u>Ibid</u>., p. 398.

First century ideas were born under the aegis of a flat-earth cosmology with its tripartite universe: heaven above, hell beneath, and humans midway in between.

When that cosmology changed, as it did following the Copernican Revolution and the subsequent Enlightenment, all those earlier notions necessarily changed along with the new framework. The person who refused to re-conceive earlier ideas in light of the modern world view became an anachronism.

Today, a flat-earth person may concede that the earth is round (spherical), but still thinks out of the first century cosmology. For that person, it is as if nothing had really changed as a result of the cosmological upheaval due to the rise of Modern Science.[5] Such a person has not yet grasped the significance of the events that shaped the Modern Mind. It is like the old joke about two fencers. The first took a quick slashing blow with his rapier to the neck of his opponent, who said, "Ha! You missed." The first fencer replied, "Oh, yeah? Shake your head."

The medieval cosmology effectively took a death-blow from the new science; however, some people are still unaware of the significance of that fatal blow. They think that they can go on believing the same old things just as if nothing had ever happened. Not so! Everything necessarily changed with the new cosmology. It was not just an event in astronomy that took place. A new paradigm came into being—a totally new way of perceiving things.

For example, the medieval person thought that the stars moved from east to west in the heavens; but the Modern Mind knows otherwise. It was earth rotating on the axis that gave the appearance that the stars moved. Humans, along with their earth, were the ones who were moving. The

---

5   For details on the Seven Salvos of Science, see pp. 37-41 in chapter IV.

so-called "celestial motion" was relative to their earth-bound perspective.

That is the metaphor for the entire modern world view. Everything in the modern world is relative to one's perspective. There is no absolute stand-point from which all else can be judged. Albert Einstein's Special and General Theories of Relativity have demonstrated once and for all the modern man lives in a relativized universe. "Everything is relative; and only that is absolute," wrote Auguste Comte.

This is not the place to argue the merits of such a relativized worldview. It suffices to note that there has been a collapse of meaning in the Postmodern World. The consequences of such a relative universe are profound in that having destroyed the belief in absolutes, many are left adrift without any moorings. They have nothing which might provide a solid basis for a comprehensive and meaningful universe. Consequently, once more they are faced with the abyss of both the inner and outer voids. Life has lost its grounding for a moral imperative. Richard Tarnas has described the human predicament in the following manner:

> [We receive] two messages from our existential situation: on the one hand, strive, give oneself to the quest for meaning and spiritual fulfillment; but on the other hand, is acutely indifferent to that quest, soulless in character, and nullifying in its effects. We are at once aroused and crushed. For inexplicably, absurdly, the cosmos is inhuman, yet we are not. The situation is profoundly unintelligible.[6]

We have briefly reviewed how two main anxiety producing forces—death and meaninglessness—have confronted individuals with the boundless void. Attempts

---

[6] Ibid., p. 420.

have been made by some to rationally understand and contain the void and its affects on human consciousness; but all attempts to reduce that which is inherently irrational to a meaningful, manageable rational system are doomed to failure. One is constantly frustrated and defeated in that effort. Humans naturally feel threatened by the void because it represents the negation of existence and all that makes life possible. This includes even the value system that holds human society together. Consequently, whenever the void is mentioned, people feel uneasy. They are at a loss for words and do not know how to respond; therefore, they quickly shift the conversation to something less threatening. There are two things one is not supposed to discuss at a party: religion and politics. One can add to that list a third topic—the <u>void</u>! It is a real conversation stopper at a cocktail party. Humans avoid the void like a plague.

Rather than fleeing from the void, people need to face it and learn how to live with it. It is everyone's destiny. But this need not immobilize the individual. Life can be energized by the knowledge that one is finite and that one does not have unlimited time. Knowledge of this affords the opportunity to reassess one's values in light of the fact that one won't live forever; then, the individual can choose to live with maximum effectiveness in the time one has left.

A quick overview of this study reveals that there are countless ways that one might encounter the void. The two that have been discussed so far—death and meaninglessness—are probably the most prevalent; however, subsequent chapters will indicate numerous other avenues of encounter.

I have divided the study into two main parts: <u>The Outer Void</u> and <u>The Inner Void</u>. There is a third part that deals with <u>Filling the Inner Void</u>, but that is really a subsidiary section to the <u>Inner Void</u>.

The outer, or external void, deals with the void as encountered outside of the human psyche. It takes two principal forms: <u>temporal</u> and <u>spatial</u>. The temporal void has to do with human history at both ends of the timeline; whereas, the spatial void has to do with the physical universe—both large and small.

The <u>Temporal Void</u> deals with <u>primordial time</u>, i.e., the <u>primeval past</u>. One finds that type in the Creation narratives and mythological lore of all ancient cultures. On the other hand, it is also met at the extreme opposite end of the timeline in the <u>eschaton</u>, or <u>future denouement</u> of human history. That chapter deals with the void in a temporal context both in terms of the ancient mythical accounts and the modern scientific notion of the universe in its genesis and ultimate dissolution. Thus human existence is bounded at both ends by nothingness—by the eternal void.

The <u>Spatial Void</u> has to do with empty space in the physical universe, or non-being. It is encountered in two primary ways: as <u>infinitely large</u> and the <u>infinitesimally small</u>. The first has to do with the void of "outer space", or the "deep field" of the Cosmos; whereas, the second has to do with the universe on the subatomic level, i.e., the makeup of matter, the primary building blocks of the physical universe such as atoms, electrons, protons, quarks, hadrons, W and Z particles, etc. At both ends of the spectrum—the infinitely large and the infinitesimally small—one is met with the same indefinable nothingness, the spatial void. We all live inside the void.

The second part of the book, <u>The Inner Void</u>, deals with the void within the human soul. Thus the study makes a transition from living <u>inside the void</u> to the <u>void inside</u>. The metaphorical usage of the term <u>void</u> describes a universal experience common to humankind in all ages and cultures. It is that vague and undefined inner sense that something is missing—something of immense importance for a fulfilled and happy life. This second, or metaphorical usage, is the principal focus of the book. The examination of the internal void begins with a quick overview of ancient motifs about the inner void in: Jewish, Greek, Christian and Buddhist traditions; then, it turns to contemporary examples of the inner void taken from the arts (both visual and performing), literature and existential philosophy. In all cases, one is met with the pervasive sense of emptiness, hollowness and absurdity symbolized by the sculptures of Henry Moore which exhibit massive human figures with a "hole" in the torso.

The study then turns to an in-depth look at the **Grandeur and Misery of Man**. It goes to the cause of the human malaise, which we have termed <u>the inner void</u>. The chapter on **Sizing the Inner Void** in this section completes the analysis of the problem of the void—both outer and inner.

The next major section of the book has to do with human attempts to come to terms with the inner void. It is entitled, **<u>Filling the Inner Void</u>**. It outlines several strategies that have been used to deal with the inner void. First, under the heading of **Finite Answers**, it examines pleasure, wealth, fame, power, knowledge and philanthropy. Next, the survey turns to ultimate, or **Religious Answers.** Representative traditions and their solutions to the human predicament include: Greek, Christian, Hindu and Buddhist religions.

Finally, the study concludes the survey with several contemporary examples of how one might deal with the inner void in a non-religious context. That section, called **Secular Answers**, attempts to assess the merits and demerits of secular humanist solutions. The results are largely negative, except for the chapters on **Ethical Humanism or the Ethic of Inquiry** and **The Beautiful Life**. This is a bit of seminal research into the ethical dimension of the human psyche. It indicates that there is a bedrock starting point within the human situation that forms the basis for a universal, existential, stand-alone ethic, which provides humankind with grounds for a positive response in an otherwise absurd and impersonal universe. The last chapter entitled, **The Beautiful Life**, attempts to show what an authentic life lived out of first principles would look like.

In conclusion, there is no aspect of life that is not affected by the void. A person's life is bounded on all sides by it. It is pervasive, surrounding everyone; it is also invasive, penetrating the human soul. Our goal in this study is to plumb the depths of the psyche, to bring the unconscious to consciousness, to find out what humans crave, long for and require. If one could fully understand the inner void, then one would be able to fathom the depths of the human soul, and vice versa.

Those are the key points of the study. Now, the reader is invited to connect the dots along with the author and see what picture emerges. He or she is invited to join in the universally human quest for self-understanding. Perhaps, the reader will find it beneficial in understanding his or her own gnawing need—that aching void within each human heart.

Chapter II

THE CONCEPT OF THE VOID

The term *void* is often used, but seldom understood. What is meant by the void? There are common usages of the term. The word *void* can be used as a noun, verb or adjective. The verb form is perhaps the most familiar, especially as used in legal parlance. Everyone knows what it means to have a check voided. When we write the word **VOID** in big letters across the face of a check that announces it has been cancelled. It is no longer considered legal tender; hence it is non-cashable and worth nothing. It has been emptied of any monetary value.

Occasionally, the court will render a transaction "null and void". These are two words which mean essentially the same thing.[7] It means that the transaction has been rescinded. Once voided, it is nullified and no longer in effect. It has been rendered without legal force, and henceforth, considered invalid. A similar meaning is expressed when a prior order has been "vacated" by the court. It has been emptied of any obligation to comply with the order.

The term also can be used in a physical sense—both as a verb and as a noun. In a scientific laboratory, one evacuates or voids the air from a vacuum chamber by means of an air

---

[7]   Brian A. Garner, ed. <u>Black's Law Dictionary</u>, 7th ed. (St. Paul, Minnesota: West Group, 1999). See "null" entry, p. 1095.

pump. What remains in the chamber is a vacuum, or void: it is the absence of all matter.[8] It is this latter usage of the ***void*** as a noun expressing the absence of all matter that concerns this study.

The average person seldom thinks about the ***void***; but when persons do, they find it baffling and virtually impossible to define. The void is the vaguest of all concepts because it refers to nothing, i.e. <u>no</u>-thing. One needs to have a clear idea about the void, but there is nothing clear about "nothing". How does one define the indefinable? It is like the cipher "zero". The zero is symbolized by a circular or oval ring encompassing nothing (**O**).[9]

In mathematics, the zero can represent powers of ten as long as it is preceded by an ordinal or cardinal number. If one has a monthly salary of five figures, e.g. $10,000, then one has spendable income. However, if those five figures are all zeros, then one has <u>no</u> income. No matter how many zeros one attaches to it, even if it contains an infinite number of zeros, the sum is still zero.

In mathematics, the symbol for infinity is a figure eight on its side (∞), a curved line that loops endlessly back upon itself. The zero and the infinite are limiting concepts. They represent two polar opposites of reason operating at its outer

---

[8] In quantum mechanics, absolute nothingness, as in complete nothingness, is an empty concept because it is unattainable in practice. See Marcello Gleiser, <u>The Dancing Universe</u> (New York: Penguin Putnam Books, Inc., 1997), p. 307.

[9] The Romans had no symbol for zero in their numerical system. The Arabs were the first to introduce both concept and symbol of the zero. Hence, the Western system of counting employs Arabic numerals. The word *zero* comes from the Arabic word *sifr*. According to the historian Will Durant, this "circle the Moslems called <u>Sifr</u>, 'empty' whence [comes] our *cipher*. Latin scholars transformed *sifr* into *zephyrm*, which Italians shortened into zero." <u>The Age of Faith</u>, p. 241 (New York: Simon and Schuster, 1950).

limits—at the furthermost edge of its ability to process rational thought. The void is often referred to as the "infinite void", because it is unbounded and without limit.

The void represents the absence or lack of everything— which is nothingness; as such, it is the darkest of all negatives. It negates everything that makes existence possible. It is abysmal and equivalent to the philosophical term non-being. That which is has being; whereas, that which is not is called non-being. Non-being is the negation of all that is; it the antithesis of being.

It is difficult for some people to grasp abstractions; and the void, or non-being, is the most abstract of all terms. The concept of the void is so vague and abstract that most people give up thinking about it altogether. It is too difficult for them. They are accustomed to dealing with the pragmatic objects and events of everyday life. When lecturing on the topic of being to a group of lay persons, I often get a blank stare; but when the term non-being is introduced, their eyes glass over and I know that I have lost them entirely.

I find that the easiest way to explain the concepts of being and non-being to lay persons is to talk about "coffee and doughnuts". Everyone is familiar with the circular pastry called a "doughnut". The round pastry has a hole cut out of its center before the dough is dunked into hot oil. The finished product is a light airy pastry in the shape of a ring (torus). This edible cake-like pastry is comparable to being, because it has substance that can be seen, touched, tasted and eaten. The doughnut ring has its distinctive shape because it is surrounded by empty space, both inside and out. The empty space is what is referred to as non-being. Both being and non-being are essential for the doughnut to retain its familiar torus shape. Both concepts are necessary to describe an object like a doughnut.

It has been stated that the void (non-being) is the vaguest of all concepts; as such, it is the most abstract and empty of all terms. It is indefinable because it has no form or limits. Taken by itself, it is a meaningless term. If all were non-being (nothing), then nothing would have any meaning. Likewise, if all were <u>being</u>, then no distinctions would be possible. Everything would be equally, everywhere and uniformly the same. Thus the terms <u>being</u> and <u>non-being</u> are correlative terms, neither of which can stand alone. One has no meaning without the other. It is like the line from the musical stage play, <u>Oklahoma</u>: "Love and marriage, horse and carriage . . . you can't have one without the other."

Non-being is a negative that has meaning only in relation to a positive; yet non-being is the negation of all that is positive. Moreover, the negative is necessary in order for the positive to have any meaning. It's a paradox!

A good illustration about the correlation between being and non-being comes from the Spanish philosopher Miguel Unamuno in his book, <u>The Tragic Sense of Life</u>. He relates the story of an artillery sergeant who was asked by a new recruit how cannons were made. The sergeant replied, "First, you take a hole; and then, you wrap steel around it." This humorous anecdote illustrates the absurdity of talking about non-being as if it were an entity in-and-of-itself. Holes do not exist except in relation to something of substance surrounding it.

The terms <u>being</u> and <u>non-being</u> were coined by the ancient Greek philosophers like Parmenides, Heraclitus and Democritus. They founded the science of ontology. The Greek word for <u>being</u> is <u>ontos</u>; hence ontology is the knowledge and study of being. The Greeks puzzled over the questions: what does it mean to <u>be</u>? What is the nature of Being? What is the makeup of the cosmos?

The age-old problem of being and non-being arose when philosophers like Leucippus and Democritus tried to picture the world as made up of tiny indivisible units of matter that they called <u>atoms</u>. Democritus proclaimed that nothing exists but "atoms and the void", and that the atoms move, not according to the will of an intelligent being, but through an impersonal force of law. These atoms, for Democritus were analogous to extremely small, but discrete, particles qualitatively identical, but differing in size and shape. Each of the infinite number of particles of matter were separated from the other by space, or non-being. They bounced around in empty space forming various combinations. Different combinations of atoms gave different properties, but essentially the basic material of the world was made of the same fundamental atomic particles.

Today, of course, particle physicists know that the basic building blocks of matter are infinitely more complex than the ancient Greek model. Nevertheless, the Greek model illustrates quite well how being and non-being are correlative concepts that cannot stand alone.

One might not consciously be aware of the void, i.e. non-being, but it is the basis and <u>a priori</u> presupposition of all human existence. It is like breathing air; the respiratory system continues to operate whether or not one is conscious of it. Being, and its correlate, non-being, are the basis for all that is. It makes human reality possible.

In summary, the concept of the void includes both outer and inner voids. In the above paragraphs, the outer void was defined in terms of the physical world as the emptiness, or absence of matter. It is the nothingness, or non-being of empty space which, as has been noted, has meaning only in correlation to that which has being or substance. However, the principal meaning of the term <u>void</u> in this study has to do with its metaphorical usage as the <u>inner void</u>. When we speak of the <u>void in the human soul</u>, we are using the term in an existential, symbolic sense to refer to the individual's awareness of an emptiness or hollowness that is felt within the self. Something vital, something necessary to live a full and complete life is absent. It will be the goal of the second half of this inquiry to find out what that missing element is.

It will not be necessary to go into great detail about the metaphorical sense of the void at this juncture, because that is the primary focus of the entire study. It suffices simply to note the difference between the physical and metaphorical usages.

Chapter III

TEMPORAL VOID

1. The Primeval Past

The **Outer Void** is encountered in two principal ways: as the **temporal** and **spatial** voids. With regard to the temporal mode, the void can be observed at both ends of the timeline, i.e., at the beginning and end of world time. It is met at the **origin** or **genesis** of the world; and at the **eschaton** or **final denouement** of world history. In the first instance, one finds the void in the Creation narratives of most ancient cultures. It is generally cast in the form of a primal state of chaos and darkness; or, a watery, amorphous state.

In the Greek tradition, Hesiod, in his <u>Theogony</u> wrote,"First, Chaos came, and then broad-bosomed Ea—the everlasting seat of all that is."[10] Chaos was another way of referring to the <u>void</u>. Thus out of chaos came a cosmos. The term <u>kosmos</u> is the Greek word for "order". An ordered world emerged out of disorder and chaos, i.e., out of the void.

In the Hebrew Creation narrative, it states that the world originally was "without form and <u>void</u>." The two key Hebrew

---

[10] Hesiod quoted by Paedrus in Plato's <u>Symposium</u> in <u>The Works of Plato</u>, Edwin Irwin, ed., (New York: McGraw-Hill, Inc., 1956), p. 341.

words are <u>behon</u> (form) and <u>tehon</u> (void).[11] It is important to note that in Hebraic thought, as in Greek, the void preceded all that is, i.e., all that has created form or being. In the Jewish writing, <u>The Wisdom of Solomon</u>, it states that the Lord "fashioned the universe from formless matter."[12]

Typically, ancient peoples depicted the origins of the world in the language of myth, i.e., in terms of pictorial and metaphysical symbols—often expressed in terms of the cosmic dragon of chaos. Our ancestors had both a fascination for, and fear of, dragons. These mythic monsters represented all that was chaotic, destructive and hostile in Nature. Ancient maps exhibited large land masses that had not yet been explored. Across the face of these areas mapmakers wrote these words: <u>Terra Incognito</u>, and often added these words or warning—<u>There be Dragons!</u> Anyone foolish enough to venture into their forbidden realm was courting disaster.

Those imaginary beasts represented an incarnation of chaos; and for that reason, ancient, cosmogonic myths (myths of origin or creation of the world) depicted this <u>animal horribilis</u> as the primeval force of chaos and disorder that had to be overcome before an ordered world in which humans could dwell would be possible. In many ancient Creation narratives, the cosmic dragon had to be fought in a fierce battle and defeated before a cosmos could come into being.

In the Babylonian creation narrative <u>Enuma elis</u>, the primal dragon gods, Apsu and Tiamat, were depicted as the original source of all gods and human beings. In the economy of symbolism, they also represented the male and female principle, as well as the primal waters of Apsu (sweet water) and Tiamat (salt water). Ancient mythic symbols were often multi-valent and took on a variety of meanings. Assyriologists

---

[11]   Brown, Driver, Briggs, <u>Hebrew-English Lexicon</u>, see entry tehon.

[12]   <u>Wisdom of Solomon</u>, 11:17.

surmise that the biblical term for the void, <u>tehon</u>, was a linguistic derivative of the Babylonian <u>Tiamat</u>.

In the Babylonian Creation account, Apsu and Tiamat spawned a family of gods that grew rapidly and became so noisy and disruptive that Apsu complained to Tiamat that it would be necessary to destroy their progeny. At first, Tiamat was appalled at the thought; however, when the other gods got wind of the plot, they banded together and slew Apsu. This so enraged Tiamat that she declared war on the lesser gods. She created an army of dragons and other monsters to fight on her behalf.

The lesser gods, once again, banded together and chose the strongest and bravest among them, a god named Marduk. Marduk prepared for war by gathering his weapons and enlisting the help of the powerful north wind. They engaged Tiamat in battle and the north wind blew so fiercely that it caused the open maw of Tiamat to widen into an open cavern. Then Marduk shot his arrows into her mouth, striking Tiamat's heart and killing her.

Marduk was proclaimed chief god among all the gods. He split the body of Tiamat in half, using part to create the celestial heavens and part to create the earth. According to the <u>Enuma elis</u>, Marduk then created the sun, moon and stars to give light and mark time (e.g., there were four seven day phases of the moon to mark the four weeks of the lunar month). Marduk also created plants and animals. With the help of the female goddess Aruru, humans were created out of the blood of the slain god Kingu, one of the gods defeated along with Tiamat. Thus out of chaos came a cosmos. Again, an ordered world emerged out of disorder and chaos, i.e., out of the void.

Remnants of this myth are found in the Hebrew Bible in the books of Job, Psalms and Isaiah.[13] The theme about the slaying of the dragon of chaos at the beginning of time in order to establish cosmic order occurs in a number of ancient religious traditions.

In the Canaanite religion, one finds another dragon tale. The god of rainfall and fertility named Baal, subdues Yam, god of the sea, and defeats Leviathan, a sea dragon, who is also called Rahab. Baal thus gains control of the weather and seasons and brings about order to the world. Specialists in ancient Near Eastern texts have noted that the Canaanite dragon has the same name as the dragon of the Bible. In the Book of Psalms, there is a description of how Yahweh entered into a cosmic struggle with the sea monster, Leviathan, associated with primal chaos.

> You divided the sea by your might;
> You broke the heads of the dragons on the waters.
> You crushed the heads of Leviathan.[14]

---

[13] See Job 26:13; 41:1; 7:12; Isaiah 27:1; 51:9; Psalm 74:13-14; 89:10; 104:26; Job 41. The author of Job describes the sea dragon Leviathan in vivid language: "His snorting throws out flashes of light; his eyes are like the rays of dawn. Firebrands stream from his mouth; sparks of fire shoot out. Smoke pours from his nostrils as from a boiling pot over a fire of reeds. His breath sets coals ablaze, and flames dart from his mouth . . . ." The author is so eager to show that Elohim was not preceded by any other being that he has Elohim boasting that he created the mythological dragon of chaos—an animal horribilis that was a product of human imagination.

[14] Psalms 74:13-14.

The Hebrew prophet Isaiah echoes the same dragon myth. He exclaims of Yahweh,

> Was it not you who cut Rahab to pieces,
> Who pierced the dragon?
> Was it not you who dried up the sea,
> The waters of the great deep?[15]

Students of comparative religion have pointed out that it is no coincidence that this same dragon-slaying myth appears both in the Canaanite religion and the Bible. The Hebrews invaded the land of Canaan and adopted many of its customs and myths, according to their own admission.[16]

There is another dragon tale in Greek mythology. The god Zeus rebelled and attacked his father Cronus and the Titans (brothers of Cronus). He also slew the fire-breathing monster Typhon; however, he left it to his son Apollo to dispatch the huge primal serpent dragon Python, who menaced the universal order. Zeus was a sky god who controlled the weather and was known for his justice and protection of the home. A cosmos was once again preserved from chaos by defeating the dragon of chaos and disorder.

In India, the Rig Veda relates the myth of how the storm god Indra armed with the thunderbolt defeated Vitra, the dragon of chaos and brought cosmic order (rita)to the world. However, it was the god Varuna who maintained the cosmic order and established justice.

The Egyptians recounted a Creation myth where all was originally darkness and water; the god Nu (Nun) was the primordial water. Nu alone existed; then, out of the waters arose the primeval hillock of land. This newly born land was the world. It was dry land surrounded by an infinite sea of

---

15   Isaiah 51:9.
16   Psalms 106:35-38.

water (representing the void). So, once more in the ancient myths, order arose out of chaos.

The Egyptians also had a myth about the cosmic struggle between the sun god <u>Re</u> and the evil dragon of chaos <u>Apophis</u> (<u>Apop</u>) located in the underworld. This mythological tale recounts, not only the primordial encounter of these two powerful forces at the beginning of time; it also depicted it as a daily occurrence. The sun god <u>Re</u> expended its energy during the diurnal voyage across the heavenly vault in its golden barque. At the end of the day, it returned from the West to the East via an underground river. While making this nightly voyage, it "recharged its batteries", so to speak. While this was transpiring, it was attacked by the dragon <u>Apop</u> who tried to destroy the sun and return the world to chaos. The god <u>Seth</u> did battle on behalf of <u>Re</u> and cut the serpent dragon into pieces. Thus, a safe journey was secured for the sun god <u>Re</u> to once more continue its journey to give light and replenish the earth.

Should <u>Apop</u> ever win the battle, the world would be plunged into the darkness of the void; therefore, each night Egyptian priests would perform rituals to restore power to <u>Re</u> and insure a safe journey. This recurring primordial myth to contain the cosmic dragon of chaos and maintain order was but another example of the ancient world's attempt to conquer and control the threat of the void. In this myth about the dragon <u>Apop</u>, one not only has a myth of the past, but also, one that affected the future of Egyptian society on a daily basis; hence, it spans both past and future.

In a sense, the modern scientific theory about the origin of the universe is not too different from these ancient myths. The "Big Bang" theory posits a universe that emerged out of a primordial explosion emanating from a single point in the vast nothingness of space (that is, if space-time had any meaning prior to "the Event"). In other words, the cosmos came out of a void of nothingness. The theory of an expanding universe out of the Big Bang is not some cockamamian theory dreamed up by some dillusionary, mad scientist. It is dictated by a rational and mathematical extrapolation backwards from observations of the receding galaxies first made and documented by the pioneering astronomer Sir Edwin Hubble in the 1920s.

2. Future Denouement

Similar myths are told about what happens at the other end of the timeline of world history. At the Eschaton, or the anticipated "end of the world," there is pictured a final battle with the forces of evil, once again, symbolized as the cosmic dragon of chaos and disorder. In that climactic struggle, the dragon meets its final defeat. Isaiah, in the Hebrew Bible, depicts these events associated with the Last Day of Judgment: "For behold the Lord comes out of his place to punish the inhabitants of the earth for their iniquity."[17] As part of this final denouement of history, the destruction of the cosmic dragon called "Leviathan" takes place.

> In that day the Lord with his severe sword, great
>   and strong,
> Will punish Leviathan the fleeing serpent,
> Leviathan that twisted serpent;
> And he will slay the reptile that is in the sea.[18]

Leviathan, as has been noted, appears elsewhere in the Hebrew Bible as the primordial dragon that Yahweh defeated establishing order in the world.

The next dragon story that shall be examined comes from the vision of John in <u>The Revelation</u>. No one can accuse John of Patmos of a lack of imagination. In his account of

----

[17]   Isaiah 26:21.
[18]   Isaiah 27:1.

the final denouement of human history, he described how the archangel Michael and his angels would engage the great, fiery red dragon with seven heads in a final battle between the forces of good and evil. The struggle began in heaven where the tail of the red dragon swept a third of the stars of heaven out of their places in the dome of heaven and flung them down to earth.[19]

Perhaps, there is no clearer evidence of the primitive tripartite cosmology than this passage. The stars were conceived as being like so many shiny Christmas tree ornaments in the dome of the sky that could be dislodged and thrown down to earth. There was a total lack of understanding about what stars are, or the size and constitution of the universe. The battle between the cosmic dragon of chaos and the angel Michael, which began in heaven, ended with the dragon and his forces being cast down to earth. The dragon was identified as "that serpent of old, called the Devil and Satan, who deceives the whole world."[20]

Once again, the mythic dragon of evil and chaos, which represents the void, threatened the whole of humanity. As it had to be defeated in the cosmic battle at the beginning of time, so it must now be finally destroyed at the end of time. Its destruction prepared the way for a new heaven and a new earth, which would emerge with John's utopian vision of the "holy city" coming down from the clouds—a city free from all chaos and disorder.

The final battle, which began in heaven and ended on earth, resulted in the final defeat of evil and the establishment of the kingdom of God on earth where righteousness would reign. Satan and his minions would be thrown into the lake of fire in the deepest netherworld and burn there forever. The images of "Hell" and "chaos" are symbols of the void, which

---

[19]   Revelation 12: 3-4.

[20]   Revelation 12: 9.

is the state of existence apart from all that is life-affirming. "Hell" will be examined later in this study.

Dragon imagery is also found in the eschatological myths about the "end of the world" in Zoroastrian religion. The dragon Azhdahak is identified with evil, as elsewhere. In the Final Days, the dragon must be slain so that good might triumph once-for-all over evil. This would allow the savior, Saoshyans, to return to earth, initiating the resurrection and Final Judgment. Zoroastrianism is important because scholars are agreed that it had an immense influence on Judaism, Christianity and Islam. The innovation of the idea of Satan comes from Zoroastrianism.

The notion of personified evil, or Satan, appears in the Hebrew Bible only after their contact with Zoroastrianism during the Exile, while the Jews were being held captive in Babylon. This can be observed clearly in the pre-exilic passage where David is instructed by Yahweh to take a census of the people of Israel and then is angry at David for doing so.[21] In a parallel account written after the Exile, it is Satan that tempts David to take a census of the people, and Yahweh is therefore angry with David for doing so.[22] A severe theological problem was solved by introducing the notion of Satan as David's tempter, rather than God.

Other elements of Zoroastrianism that influenced Judaism, Christianity and Islam were the teachings of the Savior or Deliverer to come, the elaborate angelology and demonology, a final resurrection, Divine Judgment and immortality in the afterlife.

The Nordic peoples had a similar myth about a sea dragon, Jormungand, the Midgard Serpent that lived at the bottom of the ocean and which was responsible for roiling the waters, which created great waves and deadly storms so

---

[21]   II Samuel 24:1, 10, 15, 16 (Pre-exilic text).
[22]   I Chronicles 21:1, 7, 8 (Post-exilic text).

greatly feared by that sea-going people. Jormungand was the offspring of Loki, the trickster god, and his giantess consort.

In Norse mythology, the end of all things would come in a day called Ragnarok, which was the final battle between the gods, human beings, giants and monsters. Odin, the All-father god, had foreseen that the gods were doomed to perish in Ragnarok. On that day, the sea monster Jormungand would rise from the sea and do battle with the god Thor. Thor, with his magic hammer Molinir, would slay the Midgard Serpent, but he too would die in the conflict, as would all the gods. Everything would be destroyed and it would be the end of all things. However, the Norsemen believed that out of the sea would grow again the new world and a new human race where there would be peace and harmony. And they believed that out of the ashes of the old world would arise another race of gods, where would reign joy, peace and eternal happiness.

These myths of Judaism, Zoroastrianism, Christianity and the Norse religion, all recount the story of a world that emerged out of chaos, but not entirely. According to them, the cosmic dragon of chaos would have to be defeated once more—this time forever, and the human race would then live in peace and harmony. Thus chaos was at the origin of the world in the form of the cosmic dragon of chaos, and at the Eschaton with a Final Battle that defeats the dragon of chaos once-and-for-all. The ultimate hope and dream of humanity was the total defeat of all chaos and disorder.

Why did these myths—both primeval and future oriented—come into being? What in the human psyche requires such fanciful answers to the human predicament? One must recognize the awful aloneness and helplessness that humans feel in face of the naked void. Myths offer a comprehensive answer to the ever-present threat. They turn unanswered questions into satisfying comprehensive solutions that can be comprehended by the masses. Like fairy tales, they turn unpleasantness into a happy ending. That is why myths were created.

For the true believer, the myths remain unbroken. They represent true reality. The believer cannot get outside of the myth and become objective and criticize it. Therefore, he or she cannot grasp what is going on in myth-making.

But for those who recognize it as a broken myth, *i.e.,* one which has symbolical value, but is not to be taken literally, they are able to transcend the myth and to use their critical faculties to evaluate its merits and demerits. Myths have their value as a means of expressing the inexpressible, but always within metaphorical limits. As Plato once wrote in the Phaedo regarding myths of immortality: [If it is not] "exactly true, . . . [one] may venture to think, not improperly or unworthily, that something of the kind is true."[23] Plato was intellectually flexible enough to recognize the limitations of human knowledge and the need for myth to express the inexpressible.

For modern cosmologists, the future of the universe is not depicted in such glowing and positive terms. They describe the end of the expanding universe in terms of the gradual blinking out of the lights as galaxies recede farther and farther into the darkness of deep space. The Milky Way galaxy will be alone and eventually burn out. All that is left will be the icy blackness of a dead universe. What is our final destiny? Science projects the "Big Freeze," i.e., a return to the primordial chaos of the void.[24]

---

[23]   Plato, Phaido, in Irwin, op.cit., p. 185.

[24]   There is an alternative theory: Instead of continuous expansion, the universe would cease expanding and collapse back into the primal fireball out of which it emerged. That is called "The Big Crunch". However, present calculations indicate that there is not enough mass in the universe to cause a gravitational slowing and collapse. At any rate, the final result would be the same for humanity, i.e., oblivion—a return to the void.

What can one conclude from all of this? Temporally, the void is found at the beginning and at the end of time, at the genesis and final dissolution of the universe. It will once more return to that ultimate void of nothingness out of which it emerged.

Individuals know of a time when they were not, and a time when they will not be. Their lives are lived in a brief space of time bounded at both ends by nothingness. As they came out of the void, so they go back into the void. As Vladimir Nabokov expressed it: "[O]ur existence is but a brief crack of light between two eternities of darkness."[25]

The same can be said about the universe—it exists within a temporal void that had no discernible beginning and has no discernible end.

---

[25]   Vladimir Nabokov, <u>Speak, Memory</u> (1942), ch. 1.

Chapter IV

SPATIAL VOID

1. Infinitely Large

Contemporary humans live in the Space Age characterized by an open, infinite universe. However, that conception of the universe is a relatively recent phenomenon. The transition from a closed, finite universe to an open, infinite universe is a story worth retelling because it illuminates the role of the void in modern cosmology.

Most ancient cultures espoused a closed, finite universe with earth as its stationary center. For example, the ancient Greek cosmology of Homer and Hesiod was that of a flat, round disk surrounded by Oceanus, the watery limit of earth, with the sky gods dwelling above it all. The same world picture can be observed in the writings of the biblical prophet Isaiah:

> It is he [Yahweh] who sits above the circle of the earth, and its inhabitants are like grasshoppers, who stretches out the heavens like a curtain and spreads them out like a tent to dwell in.[26]

---

[26] Isaiah 40:22.

The view of the earth as flat, round disk, representing the circle of the horizon was common in ancient cosmologies, as was the idea of the heavens as a canopy, or dome, over the flat earth. Beyond the dome was the realm of the gods, the Empyrean Heavens. The structure of those cosmologies was carefully defined. It was a tripartite world with heaven above, the netherworld beneath, and earth in between. Earth was at the center of the cosmos. Even later, after the Greek philosophers had determined that the shape of the earth was spherical, they still conceived the earth as the stationary center of the finite universe around which all celestial bodies orbited.

Aristotle calculated his geocentric universe to be only 185,000 miles in diameter. In other words, his concept of the universe was that of a closed, finite, measurable space with the earth at its center. An infinite space can have no center or diameter; therefore, if a cosmology has a center, it is by definition finite. Most people accepted this finite world picture; however, the atomists, like Leucippus and Democritus, ventured to postulate a universe that was infinite.

During the medieval period, scholars attempted to combine the biblical cosmology with the ancient Greek cosmology of Aristotle and Ptolemy. They constructed what has been termed the Medieval Synthesis. The classical expression of that synthesis is found in Dante's epic poem, The Divine Comedy. Dante's Comedy reflects the fact that the Church added to the geocentric cosmology an anthropomorphic dimension where the earth was not only the physical center of the universe; it was also the spiritual center and hence the center of God's continuing concern.

Biblical cosmology, with its familiar tripartite world picture, viewed God and his angelic host as populating the heavens; and Satan with his demonic minions inhabiting the netherworld. Both realms would send their emissaries onto the human stage to do battle for human souls. Salvation history was what the whole universe was all about. It was all considered part of God's plan, and to question one part was to questions the whole.

That was the worldview that existed as the time of Nicholas Copernicus and Galileo Galilei. The new science, which would challenge the Medieval Synthesis and eventually undermine its foundations was just getting under way.

Under the relentless pressure of the new science, the medieval worldview began to come apart and its foundations crumble. Science leveled seven salvos against that once proud but doomed medieval cosmology. In order to appreciate the effect of the Copernican and scientific revolutions on medieval cosmology, it will be necessary to describe the seven pillars that formed the foundation of the biblical cosmology and what I call the Seven Salvos of Science that destroyed them.

The seven pillars that formed the foundation of the biblical cosmology were largely derived from the seven day Creation narrative in <u>Genesis</u>. They were:

1. A stationary earth at the center of the tripartite universe.
2. A spiritual cause behind all physical phenomena.
3. The seven day chronology of Creation.
4. A special divine creation of humankind.
5. Human consciousness as a reflection of the <u>imago dei</u>.
6. The absoluteness and exclusivity of the biblical perspective.
7. The universe created for humankind as a stage for salvation history.

These seven pillars came under attack and were destroyed one by one as a result of the Seven Salvos of Science, leaving the once proud Medieval Synthesis in shambles.

The first salvo was a cannonball lobbed by Copernicus. Nicholas Copernicus was a Polish priest and astronomer who was concerned about the problem of planetary motion. Astronomers had wrestled with the knotty problem of explaining the erratic motions of the planets. This problem had challenged the astronomer Ptolemy (c. 140 CE) who had designed the Greek cosmological picture a thousand years earlier. The Greeks called these erratic stars <u>planetes</u>, which meant "wanderers", from which is derived our term <u>planet</u>.

Without any new data, Copernicus asked the right questions and came up with a novel solution that seemed to solve the problem of the planets. He postulated in his book <u>De revolutionibus orbium coelestium</u> (<u>On the Revolutions of the Celestial Orbs</u>, 1543 CE) that the sun, not the earth, was the center of all planetary motion. Seventy years later, when Galileo constructed a telescope and turned it on the night sky, he saw there a confirmation of the Copernican theory. The universe was heliocentric, rather than geocentric. Thus the first pillar of the biblical cosmology fell.

The second salvo was a devastating volley delivered by Rene Descartes. This French philosopher set forth the view that all physical motion in the universe could be understood in terms of rational mathematical principles. This was confirmed in part by the pioneering work of Thomas Kepler; and later, in full by Sir Isaac Newton. Newton had formulated the three laws of motion and the law of universal gravity by which the motion of all physical bodies both on earth and in the heavens could be predicted mathematically in advance. Thus the motion of the moon, planets, comets, etc., operated, not by angelic intelligences, but by natural law. The second pillar was destroyed.

The third salvo was a howitzer shell hurled by Hutton. The Scottish geologist William Hutton claimed that the age of the earth was to be measured in the millions of years, not thousands, as indicated in the Bible; and certainly, the earth was not created in seven literal days. Later, in the Modern

Era, geologists extended earth's timeline to 4.5 billion years. Once more, a key pillar of the biblical cosmology came crashing down.

The fourth salvo was a bombshell detonated by Darwin. The biologist Charles Darwin didn't invent the idea of evolution; he simply described the mechanism by which it took place and documented it with reams of evidence. The result was that humankind was the product of natural selection and not the result of a special divine creation. With this devastating blow by Darwin, there came the destruction of the notion of a Golden Age in Paradise where humans and animals lived in a state of idyllic harmony. There was no Fall from a state of perfection, only a gradual evolutionary ascent of mankind as one animal species struggling for survival among millions of other species. Man had no place of privilege and no claim to be the culmination of the evolutionary process. The human species could be eliminated and replaced, like the dinosaurs who reigned at the top of the food chain for 250 million years. With the loss of this pillar, the foundations of the biblical cosmology were seriously weakened.

The fifth salvo was a fusillade fired by Freud. The psychoanalyst Sigmund Freud showed that man's actions were largely the product of irrational forces within the unconscious, rather than by conscious, rational choice. Humans, said Freud, chose what their unconscious dictated; then, attempted to rationalize their decisions. The rational mind was not the reflection of an inner <u>imago dei</u>; rather, rational powers were the result of millions of years of development. Thus man was not even master of his own house. The fifth pillar fell.

The sixth salvo was an atomic explosion activated by Einstein. The physicist Albert Einstein in his theories of Special and General Relativity described the structure of the physical universe. With those new insights, all absolutist positions regarding time and space were exploded. There was no absolute place in this space-time continuum by which to judge all else. Everything was relative. Eventually, this position tended to undermine any absolutes whatsoever. Even the World's Great Religions evolved along with humans, and none could claim absolute priority over the others. The sixth pillar fell along with the others.

The seventh and final salvo was a hydrogen bomb delivered by Hubble. The astronomer Sir Edwin Hubble demonstrated that the universe was expanding at an extremely rapid rate in all directions spreading throughout space. By extrapolating backwards, astronomers have been able to determine that the universe is some 13-15 billion years old. The Hubble Space Telescope has been able to take deep-field pictures of how the universe looked some 13 billion years ago. It has taken that long for light traveling at the rate of 186,000 miles per second finally to arrive at earth. The universe in unimaginably large and its age is mind-boggling. The entire history of the human race is but a fly speck in comparison to the vast sweep of time comprising the age of the universe. The idea that the world and the cosmos were created for the purposes of humankind has proven patently false in this Space Age. It was just another example of human hubris and narrow provincialism. Thus the seventh and final pillar supporting the biblical cosmology collapsed and along with it the medieval cosmology.

With the closed, finite cosmology of the Medieval Synthesis shattered, humans were faced with an open, infinite universe without discernible meaning or purpose. In this new infinite universe, not only was the earth replaced by the sun as the center of all motion, the sun was also relegated to being a mediocre star located two-thirds of the distance from the center of the Milky Way galaxy, which itself was composed of some 200 billion other stars. The Milky Way galaxy is some one thousand light years across and is only one of 150 billion other galaxies in the vast, impersonal universe. Truly, humankind has entered the Space Age. We are in a centerless void of a disorientingly expanded universe.

These discoveries have brought a new awareness of the vastness of the infinite space that surrounds us. Space is so devoid of matter that if one were to travel in a straight line from earth to the nearest star, Alpha Centauri, one would not encounter enough matter to fill a thimble. Astronomers inform us that the universe is 99.9% empty space and only 0.1% physical matter. We are surrounded and encompassed by an infinite void.

The human reaction to this open, infinite universe, which destroyed the medieval world view, was expressed by the 17th century poet John Donne, "'Tis all in pieces. All coherence gone."[27] The 17th century scientist and Christian mystic Blaise Pascal aptly expressed the human response when he wrote about the centerless void of an infinitely expanded universe:

> When I view the infinite spaces of the universe where there is no center or circumference and where there is no reason to be here rather than there, I am terrified by the eternal silence of these infinite spaces.[28]

The naïve biblicism that taught that the universe was created as a home for humankind, and that the sun, moon and stars were created after the earth as lights and time-keepers for the human race, became in the Space Age a ludicrous and absurd notion. The immense age of the universe and the vast distances involved show the biblical Creation narrative about a seven day Creation to be myth without scientific or factual value.

---

[27] John Donne, <u>An Anatomy of the World. The First Anniversary</u> [first published 1611] ln. 205.

[28] Blaise Pascal, <u>Pensees</u>, 206.

With the collapse of the Medieval cosmology, the walls that contained the hostile void were breached. Once more, humankind was left exposed to the centerless void of an indifferent and disorientingly expanded universe. If any meaning were to be had, it must come from humans themselves because the infinitely large Cosmos is not a friendly place for humans outside of their atmospheric cocoon. It displays no purpose or goal to support human values.

Planet Earth is our spaceship hurtling through the vast empty void. It is our only link to a safe and secure existence in this open universe extending in all directions into the infinite void. The poet and playwright Archibald MacLeish expressed it as follows:

> There with vast wings across the canceled skies,
> There in the sudden blackness the black pall
> Of nothing, nothing, nothing—nothing at all.[29]

2. The Infinitesimally Small

If the vastness of the universe is almost devoid of matter, as cosmologists indicate, then certainly that would not be the case when one turns to the substantial, physical body we call "Earth." Nevertheless, in spite of what common sense says, particle physicists tell us that what holds true on the cosmic level also is true on the subatomic level. Both the infinitely large and the ultrasmall are comprised mostly of empty space. Most of matter is a void. On the subatomic level, modern physicists report that empty space makes up 99.9% of the nuclear world, and only 0.1% contains matter.

An atom, which is the basic building block of matter, consists almost entirely of empty space. The atom is

---

[29]   Archibald MacLeish, <u>The End of the World</u> (1926).

comprised of a compact nucleus (made up of positively charged protons and neutrally charged neurons) with tiny negatively charged electrons racing around the central core at high velocities. Electrons orbit the nucleus like a micro-miniature solar system. That is the standard model; but, whether one is dealing with particles or waves has not been determined by physicists. Electrons act both as particles and waves; hence the need for quantum physics.

According to the standard model, electrons orbit the nucleus at different distances from the core. The planetary model for the structure of the atom was first suggested by Ernest Rutherford in 1910 and confirmed by Niels Bohr. Bohr calculated the distances from the nucleus that electrons would have to travel; and then, verified it experimentally in the laboratory.

At or below the dimensions of an atom is largely empty space. At the heart of everything is nothingness. Actually, nuclear researchers are not even sure of what matter is. It is definitely not composed of those discrete, impenetrable, indivisible units of matter that the ancient Greeks envisioned. It seems to be comprised of tiny packets of energy. Albert Einstein's astounding discovery of the relation between matter and energy expressed in his world famous formula $e=mc^2$ suggests that matter and energy are interchangeable. Matter can be turned into energy, and vice versa. That formula is the basis for the nuclear utilities industry, as well as the production of nuclear weapons of mass destruction.

If matter is made up mostly of empty space, then one might ask, why can't one body pass right through another, as a ghost through a wall? It can't because atomic particles are not inert physical entities; rather, they are highly charged particles that set up a force-field. This force-field repels all objects that come near it—all, that is, except the mysterious, tiny neutrino, which is a neutral, uncharged particle. It can pass right through other objects as if they weren't even there.

In conclusion, what is true on the cosmic level of the infinitely large, is also true with its mirror opposite, the subatomic world of the infinitesimally small. A vast emptiness, or the void, constitutes the majority of the universe. Almost everything in the cosmos is comprised of nothingness. Humans are encompassed on all sides by the void. It even penetrates the very substance of one's molecular makeup. Whether on the macroscopic or microscopic levels, the void penetrates and surrounds every aspect of human reality.

It reminds one of the dialogue between Alice and the Red King in Lewis Carrol's Through the Looking Glass, when the Red King asked Alice: "What do you see?" Alice answered, "Nothing." The King, impressed, commented, "What good eyes you have!" The ubiquitous void is not here nor there—it is everywhere.

Chapter V

INSIDE THE VOID

At his juncture, it is clear that human life is bounded on all sides by the void—both temporally and spatially. It is encompassed before and behind, above and below, without and within, by nothingness. One literally is encircled by emptiness. Empty space even invades the molecular structure of one's physical body. No matter which way one turns, one is faced with the same emptiness. In short, humans live <u>inside the void</u>.

That indisputable fact is a consequence of the modern world view and its scientific cosmology. A cosmology is not something one chooses; it is a given. It cannot be changed: that is, not until some new revolutionary scientific discovery dictates its revision.

The modern cosmology with its infinite, relative universe was not a problem that our forefathers faced. It is the result of recent, rapid scientific advances in the fields of quantum physics, astrophysics, astronomy and space travel— not to mention advances in the fields of geology, biology, anthropology, genome research, etc.—all of which has tended to relativize the role of human reality on an infinite and incomprehensible cosmic stage.

The change has been sudden and massive. To give a personal example, the author was born in 1929, the very year in which Sir Edwin Hubble first announced to the world his findings about the Expanding Universe. Just imagine how that event alone has changed modern cosmology. In one lifetime, the world has experienced modern marvels such as the introduction of jet aircraft, space travel in the space shuttle, human landings on the moon, robotic landings on other planets, the 200 inch Palomar reflecting telescope, Hubble Space Telescope, the International Space Station, super novas, black holes, new planets orbiting other stars, infra-red telescopes, the world-wide internet, cracking the human genome code, cloning of animals, organ transplants, lasers, sonar, radar, FM radio, fusion, transistors, integrated circuits, micro-chips, compact disks, digital cameras, cell phones, G.P.S. (Global Positioning Satellites), electron microscopes, communication and weather satellites, fax machines, color copy machines, word processors, laptop personal computers, laser printers, scanners, particle accelerators from the cyclotron to C.E.R.N.'s large hadron collider, quarks, anti-matter, super computers, nuclear submarines, solar panels, tape recorders, laser printers, the hybrid automobile, the national super highway system, robotics, A.I. (artificial intelligence), nano technology, Ipods, virtual reality devices, LCD display screens, high density 3-D flat-screen color television, fiber optics, camcorders, polymer-based plastic goods—nylon, cellophane, neoprine (synthetic rubber), wide-screen technicolor films, discovery of the double helix of the DNA molecule, M.R.I. and C.A.T. scans, polio vaccine, artificial limbs, penicilin, synthesis of enzymes needed for life-giving protein molecules, Viagra, stem cells, sulfa drugs, artificial hearts, portable kidney dialysis machines; not to mention digital watches, microwave ovens, air-conditioning, washers/dryers, dishwashers, electric refrigerators, garbage disposals, birth-control pills, credit cards, ATM banking, frozen foods, bar code scanners, snowmobiles, snowcats, artificial snow machines, hydroplane boats, DVDs, and finally I.C.B.M.s, mass spectrometers, laser guided missiles, drone aircraft, nuclear power plants,

A-bombs and H-bombs. The list goes on and on. The reader can add scores more inventions to that list—all of which our forefathers had no knowledge and couldn't have imagined in their wildest dreams. Nevertheless, those innovations have transformed the cosmology and self-image of modern humans.

It is mind-boggling to contemplate the mammoth changes that have occurred over that last one hundred years. Scientists have literally had to rewrite the textbooks about the solar system and the universe beyond.

The consequences of the new cosmology are profound. A life entirely encompassed by an infinite void loses all reference points, both temporally and spatially. Absolute time becomes a fiction, as does spatial location. Modern humans live in an infinite universe where the center is everywhere and the circumference nowhere. Everything is relative. There is no beginning or end, no up nor down, no here nor there—we are only points on an infinite continuum about which we know virtually nothing. That is the inevitable conclusion drawn from living in the vastly expanded universe of modern astronomy.

That, for better or for worse, is the modern human situation. Humans are condemned to live <u>inside the void</u>—a void that gives no clue as to whether it has a meaning or purpose. Modern humans must learn to live in a universe where everything has become relativized.

Given that cosmic perspective, the burning question is: How should one live inside the void? But before one prematurely rushes to judgment and tries to answer that query, it might be instructive to examine how our forefathers viewed the void.

Our ancient ancestors viewed the void, not as a place where one lives, but as a place where one goes after death. The void beyond the grave has been portrayed with a variety of images in various cultures. Early images of an existence after death were cast in terms of the tripartite cosmology of a closed, finite universe. Many ancient cultures viewed the afterlife as a subterranean place where departed souls go after death—a dark, dusty, murky, bodiless and joyless existence in the netherworld. Others spoke of the void as being "cast into outer darkness" or "into the bottomless pit." Both are apt images of the void.

There are many ways to approach this topic. The one chosen by this study is to pose a question about Auguste Rodin's famous sculpture, <u>The Thinker</u>. It portrays a nude male figure in deep contemplation. The irresistible question that arises is: about what is the Thinker thinking? Does he meditate on the human predicament; or, is he contemplating the mysteries of the infinite expanding universe; or, perhaps, he is pondering Plato's eternal verities: Goodness, Truth and Beauty? Or, maybe he is just trying to remember where he left his keys.

The answer to that provocative question about what the Thinker is thinking lies, no doubt, in a little known fact about its original setting. Initially, it was one of three figures in the Tympanum—a panel over the massive bronze doors created by Rodin to celebrate the opening of the Museum of Decorative Arts in Paris. The panels on the bronze doors beneath the figure of the Thinker depict the Last Judgment as envisioned by Dante in his classic work, <u>The Divine Comedy</u>. The doors, entitled "The Gates of Hell", vividly portray the horror and desperation on the faces of those lost souls who were falling into the Inferno of Hell. Thus, according to Rodin, the Thinker ponders the ultimate destiny of humankind apart from its Divine Source. The original figure of the Thinker became the model for several massive bronze replicas fashioned later by Rodin, which were exhibited detached from its original context.

In his <u>Comedy</u>, Dante describes the words emblazoned over the Gates of Hell: "Abandon All Hope Ye Who Enter Here." With those words of warning, Dante presents his version of the void. Therefore, the Thinker contemplates the emptiness and hopelessness of life lived <u>inside the void</u>.

For the ancient Greeks, the void after death was that realm called <u>Hades</u>, which was named after the god Hades who ruled the kingdom of the dead. The Romans adopted the same basic imagery, except they named their king of the dead, Pluto. In Norse mythology, the All-father, Odin, appointed the goddess Hel to rule the netherworld, from which comes the Anglo-Saxon term <u>Hell</u>.

For the Hebrews, the netherworld was called <u>Sheol</u>, with no particular ruler until after their encounter with Persian Zoroastrianism during the Exile in Babylon. Zoroastrianism was a monotheistic religion with Ahura Mazda as the Creator God. He had his evil counterpart, Angra Mainyu (The Great Satan) who ruled over the netherworld. It was only after contact with Zoroastrianism that Judaism developed the doctrine of Satan, or Devil, as ruler of the netherworld.[30]

In the earliest conceptions of the netherworld, there was no separation between the just and the unjust. All went to one place in common. As time passed, justice seemed to demand that the netherworld be divided into two realms— one for the righteous and another for the unrighteous.

For both late Judaism and early Christianity, the notions of the netherworld were greatly influenced by two streams of thought: Persian and Greek. The Persian influence has already been alluded to; therefore, the inquiry turns to the Greek source.

The ancient Greeks had an elaborate doctrine of the afterlife involving a Last Judgment for each soul after death. This was described by Plato in the <u>Phaedo</u> (c. 350 BCE), where the departed soul would be sent to Hades after receiving its sentence. There were several levels of Hades. One level was a form of Purgatory, where the individual was

---

[30]   For further details on the development of the concept of "Satan" in Israel's thought, see p.25, Chapter III.

purged of his evil deeds and rewarded for his good deeds, before returning to his celestial homeland with the gods. Plato wrote that they would go

> to the river Achern, embarking in any vessels which they may find, are carried in them to the lake and where they dwell and are purified of their evil deeds, and having suffered the penalty of the wrongs which they have done others, they are absolved, and receive the rewards of their good deeds, each according to his deserts.[31]

Does not this sound similar to the early Roman Catholic doctrine of Purgatory, which does not appear in the Bible?[32]

On the other hand, there were those who were incorrigible, who must go to their eternal damnation. This was the lake of fire in Tartarus. It was the ultimate place of punishment in the Greek cosmology. It was located in the deepest regions of Hades in the netherworld. Homer, in the

---

[31]   Plato, Phaedo, quoted in Irwin, op. cit., p. 184.

[32]   The word Purgatory does not appear in the Bible. However, the Roman Catholic Church makes the case for an intermediate place they call Purgatory based upon an obscure text in the Jewish book of II Macabees 12:44-45 which recounts a Jewish practice of that day of praying for the dead. Using largely rational arguments, they argue that there must be a place for departed saints to "purge their sins" before entering Heaven. However, in II Corinthians 15:29, the Apostle Paul speaks of a practice of baptizing for the dead; but no similar argument is made for continuing such a practice in the Church today. Most probably, some members of the Early Church borrowed the doctrine of Purgatory from the Greek teaching of departed souls purging their sins in the lake of Achern, as described by Plato approximately 400 years before the founding of the Early Church.

8[33] century BCE described Tartarus as being, "Far off, where is the innermost depth beneath the earth."[33]

Deep in the interior of the earth was a huge chasm filled with molten lava. Tartarus was a lake of fire, wrote Plato, "that throws up jets of fire in different parts of the earth."[34] Plato compared it to the volcanic eruptions of Mount Etna in Sicily. He wrote that there surged in and out huge subterranean "rivers of fire and streams of liquid mud . . . and lava streams which follow them."[35] Tartarus was reserved for

> those who appear to be incurable by reason of many and terrible deeds of sacrilege, murders foul and violent, or the like—such are hurled into Tartarus which is their suitable destiny and never to come out.[36]

Likewise, in the Christian Bible, the Second Epistle of Peter describes the ultimate destination of the rebellious angels and the damned using the same Greek term <u>Tartarus</u> to portray the place of judgment and punishment.

> God did not spare the angels who sinned, but cast them down to hell [Greek: <u>Tartarus</u>] and delivered them into chains of darkness to be reserved for judgment.[37]

> This same theme is repeated in <u>The Revelation</u> to John.

---

[33] Irwin, <u>Ibid</u>., p. 181.

[34] <u>Ibid</u>., p. 183.

[35] <u>Ibid</u>., p. 181.

[36] <u>Ibid</u>., p. 184.

[37] II Peter 2:4.

The devil, who deceived them, was cast into the
lake of fire and brimstone where the beast and
the false prophet are. And they will be tormented
day and night for ever and ever.[38]

The Greek influence on late Judaism and Early
Christianity can also be found in the fact that the Gospel
writers report that Jesus used the Greek word <u>Hades</u> to refer
to the final place of judgment in the after-life; thus borrowing
a term from the Greek myth of Hades.[39]

These ancient images of the place of punishment for the
wicked were taken quite literally in their time, as can be seen
in the words of the prophet Amos in his warning to Israel,

Though they dig into hell (Sheol),
From there my hand shall take them
Though they climb up to heaven,
From there will I bring them down.[40]

According to Amos, one could take a shovel and literally
dig one's way into Hell (Sheol); or, one might even climb a
ladder to Heaven. The distances were not thought to be that
great in their ancient, finite cosmology.

However, all of that radically changed with the advent of
the Copernican Revolution. Suddenly, the closed, finite world
became an open, infinite universe. The modern cosmology
laid to rest once and for all the primitive tripartite cosmology
of the ancient world. Hell lost its location, as did Heaven. The
meaning of those terms necessarily changed along with the

---

[38] Revelation 20:10.

[39] Luke 19:23. Jesus of Nazareth most likely spoke Aramaic;
nevertheless, the Synoptic Gospel writers report that Jesus used
the Greek term <u>Hades</u> to refer to the place of Final Judgment
for sinners.

[40] Amos 9:2.

new, infinite and relative cosmology. No longer could those notions possess the physical coordinates of up or down. In a thoroughly relativized cosmos, it was necessary to understand those terms in a purely symbolical sense. Hell is not a place beneath the surface of the earth, nor is Heaven "up there" in the clouds. Many have still not thought through the logical consequences of the Copernican cosmology and the Scientific Revolution.

Although some still try to hang onto the ancient myth of Hell, in reality it is ignored. Hell is seldom mentioned from the pulpit these days. One does not hear sermons like that of Jonathan Edwards, "Sinners in the Hands of an Angry God." One is more likely to hear the minister or priest speak, not of Dies irae (Day of Wrath), but of the love of God. The doctrine of Hell is assiduously avoided. Thus change in the intellectual climate has brought a radical change in the way the notion of Hell is received by modern humans.

Today, one is more likely to hear the comment that we make our own Hell here on earth. For the modern mind, Hell is a state of mind, not a place to go. Jean-Paul Sartre captured that existential attitude toward Hell in his play, <u>No Exit</u>. He describes three individuals: two females and male who are shut up in a room together in Hell for all eternity. The characters are: Estelle, who is a lesbian; Innes, an infanticidist; and Garein, who is a coward, a phoney pacifist who avoids military duty. Each seeks the other's affirmation, but receives only judgment and guilt. The three begin to tear at each other and accuse each other about their crimes and weaknesses. The conflict between the three continues without abatement through all eternity. Sartre concludes that "Hell is other people."[41] Humans create their own Hell by their inner hostilities, hatreds and intolerance.

In the last analysis, everyone constructs his or her own prison. They design the cage within which they will live. They

---

[41]   Jean-Paul Sartre, <u>No Exit</u>. Sc. V.

set their own limits as to what they will permit themselves to be and do; and they seldom, if ever, think outside that box. "Denmark's a prison," said Hamlet; to which Rosencrantz replied, "Then the world is one."[42]

We all live inside the void, no matter whether it be a prison of our own making or the acceptance of one defined for us. The question for everyone becomes: How does one live inside the void? Does one succumb to hopeless dispair, or does one create a life filled with meaning? One can <u>fight</u> the void and attempt to <u>flee</u> from it; or, one can <u>face</u> it and <u>fill it with meaning</u>. How this is done is discussed in the section on **"Filling the Inner Void."**

---

42   Shakespeare, <u>Hamlet</u>, Act II, Sc. Ii, lns. 256-263.

Chapter VI

THE CONCEPT OF
THE INNER VOID

Beginning with this section, the study makes a transition from the <u>outer void</u> to the <u>inner void</u>; from the objective to the subjective; from the impersonal to the personal.

The two categories are distinctly separate, but not unrelated, because the external void becomes one's internal possibility through an event called <u>death</u>. Death is the mindless, timeless void that awaits all living beings. It is everyone's destiny. It has always been a part of the human equation; and, as such, it is not something alien. It has always been an integral part of what it means to be alive. All life terminates in death. It constitutes the unknown; hence, its threat causes anxiety; and anxiety makes the individual aware of an ongoing problem of the self—that of the <u>inner void</u>.

When one speaks of the void in the human soul, one speaks metaphorically, i.e., the image of a void in the soul portrays the experience that something is missing; there is a familiar hollowness inside. The human being is an unfinished project; it lacks completion. There is always an inner yearning for something more, something that will bring happiness and a sense of fulfillment.

People might fantasize that they would be happy if only they were to win the two-hundred-fifty million dollar powerball lottery, own a Lear jet, live in a mansion, belong to the Country Club, travel the world, wear the latest fashion, enjoy gourmet dining, vacation at San Moritz and do whatever they please. Perhaps, a person's desires might be much more modest, but the situation is fundamentally the same. There is always one more thing that one needs to be really happy and content. J. P. Morgan was once asked what it would take to make his employees happy. He replied, "A salary larger than the one they presently have."

The average person does not need to be convinced of the existence of an inner void because it is an ever-present reality and part of one's daily life. One may, or may not, be conscious of it; but it is always there like a silent phantom. It is experienced as an aching need; or more accurately, like an open wound that requires constant attention. Socrates called this urgency to attend to spiritual needs, "the care of the soul."

Some adopt the strategy of trying to ignore the inner void, hoping that it might go away; but it only resurfaces in other forms. Others deny it altogether. They would disclaim any such voidness in the soul. However, this protestation rings hollow in light of the unanimous witness of the arts, literature, drama, psychology, philosophy and religion—all of which give unambiguous testimony to the fact that humans perceive themselves as incomplete—a work in progress, a being striving for wholeness and self-realization.

It is possible that some individuals lack self-reflection and the requisite self-knowledge to recognize the inner void when it surfaces. They live such superficial lives concerned only with escapism and finite values that they are not in touch with their inner spiritual nature. They need an inner mirror that would reveal their shallowness; their lack of depth and self-understanding.

Socrates said that "the unexamined life was not worth living." For him, the first duty of each person is to <u>know myself</u>. This is not an easy task, since it takes considerable self-reflection and introspection. Thales, the Greek philosopher, was once asked to define what was difficult in life. He replied, "To know thyself." When asked what was easy, he answered, "To give advice." No wonder he was considered one of the wisest men in Greece.

In this study, we address the most fundamental questions about the human soul. We probe the depths of the soul and seek to understand the nature of the self and the endlessly fascinating world within. The human heart is an enigma, a seemingly insoluble puzzle. How does one plumb the unfathomable depths of the human soul? The human being is a mystery, a riddle, a conundrum. Who can know the labyrinthian self?

From earliest times, humans have struggled to understand the complex problem called, the self. What does it mean to be human? Who or what am I? The ancient Greeks puzzled over this problem and concluded that the human being was a duality—comprised of body (soma) and soul (psyche). The body was that outward, physical component of the self that was mortal and subject to decay; whereas, the soul was that inward, spiritual component of the self that was immortal and destined to live with the gods in Heaven. Entrance into that state of bliss depended upon how one conducted one's ethical life here on earth.

Living a virtuous life posed a problem in that the self seemed to be driven by conflicting forces. Plato expressed this in terms of a myth about a charioteer. He relates the tale about a driver whose chariot was yoked to two horses: the one was a dark, brutish and unruly beast that kept pulling to the left and throwing the chariot off course; whereas, the other was a handsome, white stallion that obeyed the driver's pull on the reins and followed his every command. The problem that the charioteer had was getting the team to work together and function as a unit. It seemed at times like an impossible task. The black beast fought and resisted any lead from the driver forcing the chariot into the ditch or in the wrong direction.

Plato compared this to the self. The charioteer represented the human will that strove to follow the path of the good life; but it had to contend with two contrary impulses in the soul—one that sought virtue; and the other, selfish and immoral interests. At times, the evil impulse would win out, which would result in self-destructive behavior. At other times, the will was in control and the finer, higher self would rule the day. The problem was to keep the self on a consistent, constructive, virtuous course.

In modern times, a similar analysis of the self has been given by the psychoanalyst Sigmund Freud—only, he gave those aspects of the self different names: the ego was the conscious, willing self; the **id** represented the cauldron of emotional and sexual instincts that vied to rule the self; and the **superego** represented parental rules and social norms that must be imposed upon the self if it is to succeed as a social being. The struggle to become individuated and whole depended upon which drives ruled the conduct of the self. The self seeks unity, completion and self-actualization; but, if it fails at that task, it becomes afflicted with neuroses, psychoses and dysfunctional behavior.

One major difference between the Freudian and Greek anthropologies was that the Freudian self was not comprised of two separate entities (body and soul); rather, it was considered a single entity with two aspects: the somatic (bodily) and the psychic (mental or soulish). The soul-body dualism was a false dichotomy. The self is always an embodied self. The psyche is not a separate entity that can be detached from the body. The self has to be treated as a unity (despite its conflicted nature).

Freud is known for his discovery of the unconscious mind and his techniques to bring the unconscious to consciousness. He was the founder of depth psychology, where the analyst probes the unconscious to locate the cause of psychic pathologies.

This study also attempts to penetrate the mystery of the self. It is an odyssey into <u>one of life's deepest mysteries—the human soul</u>. What goes on in there? What can be said about this invisible component of the self? Any adequate psychology must give an account of the insatiable self. Therefore, it is proposed that this study explore the inner workings of the soul with respect to the landscape of the human soul.

Any study that explores the void in the human soul must ask the larger question about the human condition. What lies at the source of human restlessness and dissatisfaction? It seems that humans are on a constant quest for fulfillment; but what need are they seeking to fill? What do humans really want? Why do they have a sense of incompleteness, the feeling that something is missing—something vital and necessary for human happiness? This awareness of lack or need in the human soul is what is referred to in this study as the sense of <u>inner voidness</u>.

Everyone needs an understanding of the inner void, as well as practical guidance in how to deal with it. In order to accomplish this, it will be necessary to become familiar with the scope and size of the inner void. First, it is proposed that this study look at examples of the inner void taken from the ancient world—Jewish, Greek, Christian and Buddhist. Second, examples will be given from the contemporary world of the arts (both visual and performing), literature and existential philosophy. Then, the study will examine the underlying cause of the human malaise in the section on the **Grandeur and Misery of Man**. And finally, it will attempt to measure the scope and size of the inner void.

Chapter VII

ANCIENT MOTIFS

When dealing with something so basic to human reality as the inner void, it should surprise no one that this universally human experience is found in many different cultures—both ancient and modern. It is a timeless motif. This becomes evident when we examine some representative traditions from the ancient world: first, Jewish.

1. Jewish

An example from the Jewish tradition comes from the book of Ecclesiastes in the Hebrew Bible (c. 300-200 BCE). It concerns the global indictment rendered by the author, called "Qoheleth" in Hebrew (sometimes translated as "Teacher"). The sage investigated everything that humans pursue in their quest for happiness. After performing numerous experiments in the laboratory of life, he reached the somber conclusion, "Vanity of vanities, all is vanity."[43] This statement becomes the theme of the book. Like two bookends, it appears both at the beginning and end of the book. The word vanity also appears within the text some 38 times. Vanity, without question, is the overall theme of Ecclesiastes.

---

[43] Ecclesiastes 1:2; 12:18.

Arnold C. Harms, Ph.D.

What is meant by the term <u>vanity</u>? First of all, it does not refer to egotistical, self-centered, conceited persons. The Hebrew word for vanity is <u>hebel</u>, which denotes "vapor" or "breath", something fleeting and transitory like a "mist" or "fog". A vapor or mist cannot be grasped or contained. It connotes that which is evanescent, transitory and unsubstantial. When used metaphorically, <u>hebel</u> means: empty, worthless, hollow, fruitless, aimless, having no substance, a chasing after the wind. The biblical scholar, R. B. Y. Scott, writes that <u>hebel</u>:

> Connotes what is visible, or recognizable, but unsubstantial, momentary, and profitless. The rendering must be varied to bring out the particular shades of meaning in different contexts. Thus the traditional translation, "Vanity of vanities, all is vanity" can be freely expanded to read: "<u>Everything in life is hollow and utterly futile</u>; it is the thinnest of vapors, fleeting as a breath, and amounts to <u>nothing</u>."[44] (Emphasis added)

The Jewish sage Qoehleth reported that everything he tried in life left him empty, hollow and dissatisfied. No finite value could bring him lasting happiness. Every earthly pleasure, or as he expressed it, everything "under the sun" was temporal, contingent, transitory and futile. It was a "chasing after the wind".[45] That recurrent phrase summarizes his considered judgment after tasting all of the pleasures that

---

[44] R.B.Y. Scott, "Proverbs, Ecclesiastes" in the <u>Anchor Bible</u>, (Garden City, New York: Doubleday, 1965), pp. 201,202 (emphasis added).

[45] Eccl. 1:14. The phrase, "chasing after the wind" appears some ten times in the book of Ecclesiastes to describe the human condition.

life had to offer. A similar conclusion was reached by the psalmist:

> The Lord knows the thoughts of man,
> That they are futile.[46]

Our Jewish Wisdom Teacher, Qoheleth, observed that death comes equally to man as well as animals, "all are from the dust, and all return to the dust."[47] Still, he thought it better to be alive "for a living dog is better than a dead lion. For the living know that they will die; but the dead know nothing."[48] For some, this gloomy conclusion is too pessimistic and unsatisfying, so they turn to more upbeat writings in the Bible. Others find Qoheleth's candor and realism refreshing. It reflects the hollowness and emptiness experienced by so many today. That theme is probably why the book of Ecclesiastes resonates so well with the modern mind. For the purposes of this study, the book provides an excellent illustration of an ancient Jewish encounter with the vast emptiness of the inner void.

2. Greek

In the Greek tradition, an example of the inner void is found in Plato's doctrine of Recollection. Plato's analysis of the human condition in that humans suffer from a malady called, "homesickness" of the soul. The reason for this is that they subconsciously recall a prior existence wherein they dwelt with the gods in Heaven and experienced a perfection of the Eternal Ideas: the Good, the True, and the Beautiful. Plato recounts several myths about how humans fell from

---

[46]   Psalms 94:11.

[47]   Eccl. 3:20.

[48]   Eccl. 9:4.

that idyllic state of perfection into an evil world of constant flux and turmoil, but the common element in them all was that humans still faintly remembered the ultimate source of goodness and beauty that they had experienced first-hand in their absolute form in Heaven. The scholar of platonic studies Edwin Irwin writes,

> The soul in seeing beauty is stirred to nostalgic recollection of that purer beauty, that more real beauty it had known in Heaven. The love of beauty is a <u>longing for the homeland of the soul</u>.[49] [emphasis added]

This longing for the homeland of the soul, Plato called, "homesickness". It was the experience of being estranged, cut off and alienated from one's true home and destiny. The feeling of homesickness was the awareness that life was out of joint and that one's true destiny was not on earth, but rather, in a transcendent realm with the gods.

This experience of the soul's "homesickness" is the Greek way of speaking about the inner void. There is a recognition that life is in some way deficient. It lacks fulfillment; and there is the desire that the inner void be filled. Solutions to the problem of the inner void may vary from culture to culture, but the basic problem is universal.

3. Christian

The theme of spiritual hunger in the human heart is prominent throughout the Christian religion. Jesus of Nazareth, its founder, had compassion on the multitudes who flocked around him so that he proclaimed, "Blessed are those that hunger and thirst for righteousness, for they shall

---

[49]   Irwin, op. Cit., p. xxxiii. (emphasis added)

be filled."[50] He promised fountains of living water that would quench the thirst within the soul and bring inner satisfaction and peace.

The spiritual hunger and thirst of which Jesus spoke, stemmed from mankind's sense of alienation and estrangement from its Divine Source. According to Christian teaching, humans were created to live in harmony and communion with their Creator; however, that state of innocence and bliss was shattered—not by outside forces—but as the result of evil choices made from within the human heart. As a consequence, the relationship of humanity with its Maker was disrupted, both individually and collectively, leaving a void within.

That sense of estrangement is reflected in both Old and New Testaments. The Old Testament proclaims, "There is no one that does good, not even one"[51] and in the New Testament, "All have sinned and come short of the glory of God."[52] Accordingly, Christian teaching states that this alienation was universal. The defection from the divine will result in an impaired ability to will the good. Humans, as a result of the Fall, were incapable of affecting their own salvation. The Fall was not, as with Plato, from a prior existence in Heaven, but from God and a state of perfection and bliss here on earth.

St. Augustine described the alienated condition as a state of restlessness for the divine. He wrote in his Confessions, "Our hearts are restless until they rest in thee, O God."[53] This longing in the human heart, according to Augustine, is an aching void that can only be filled by God. It is a divine restlessness that underscores the emptiness and meaninglessness of a life apart from its Maker. This divine

[50] Matthew 5:6.

[51] Ps. 14:3; Ps. 53:3; Eccl. 7:20.

[52] Romans 3:23.

[53] St. Augustine, Confessions, 1:8.

restlessness is analogous to Plato's "homesickness of the soul", a longing for one's true homeland. Once again, being estranged from one's source meant being faced with the emptiness of the void.

4. Buddhism

The Buddhist tradition also has a keen awareness of the human predicament. The Buddha's analysis of the human malaise can be found in the Four Noble Truths and the Eightfold Path. It begins with the observation that life is suffering. The Sanskrit word translated as suffering is duhkha. The term duhkha is misunderstood if it is taken only in the sense of physical pain and suffering. Duhkha is a much broader term. Suffering includes mental anguish, sorrow, disappointment, disillusionment, despair, the heartache of unrequited love and angst within the soul.

The root cause of suffering, according to the Buddha, is desire. Desire is insatiable. There seems to be no end to the desires of the human heart, and since many desires are unattainable, the result is duhkha (suffering). Even if one should attain the desired goal, desire is never satisfied. It drives one on to seek something that is bigger and better. Ultimately, there is no quenching of the fires of desire once they have been unleashed. Consequently, the end result is frustration, disillusionment and despair—in short, duhkha. The only way to avoid suffering is to eliminate desire. That is done through the Eightfold Path.

The term duhkha in Buddhist thought is analogous to the word hebel (vanity) in Jewish thought. Qoheleth's global indictment that "all is hebel" is comparable to the Buddha's proposition that "life is duhkha". Both traditions point to the anxiety that one feels in face of the void. Both have their religious and philosophical answers, which will be treated later during the course of this study.

In summary, the Jewish "vanity", the Greek "homesickness", and Christian "restlessness" and the Buddhist point to a common universal human experience of the inner void.

Chapter VIII

CONTEMPORARY MOTIFS

The themes of emptiness, meaninglessness and absurdity pervade much of the contemporary scene in art, literature and philosophy. The image of contemporary humans as being hollow, empty and having a void within the human soul has been depicted as a gaping hole in the torso. What is being expressed by that visual image? In an attempt to answer that question, examples will be taken first from the arts—both visual and performing. A quick overview of the theme of the inner void in contemporary art will be made in the fields of poetry, sculpture, painting, theater and music; then, the theme will be examined in modern literature; and finally, in existential philosophy.

1. Contemporary Art

"Every age," according to Andre Malraux, "projects its own image of man in its art." What image of man do we find in the world of modern art? There is a body of poetry, painting, sculpture, theater and music that portrays contemporary life as devoid of purpose and meaning. Artists, for better or worse, are a reflection of the collective unconscious of a culture. They give expression to the world-soul of an age. Concealed within the art are the presuppositions of a culture about the nature of humankind.

Artists, poets and literary figures frequently function as a barometer for their culture. They are sensitive to subtle changes that take place within a social fabric. They give expression to this new cultural self-understanding through their chosen medium, whether it be canvas, marble, pen-and-paper, stage, music, dance, etc. Artists often act as an early warning system for cataclysmic changes that lie ahead for a society. This prophetic role of the artist usually is something unconscious and uncontrived. It might only be observed when an art critic or art historian looks back upon a body of work and notes that certain dominant themes emerge which can be identified and analyzed.

The <u>void within</u> is one of those themes. On the macro-level, it indicates that a whole culture has undergone a fundamental change in its corporate self-understanding. The result is a deeply felt sense of loss or lack that impairs both the individual's and community's sense of identity. That which once filled a life with meaning purpose has been lost leaving a gaping wound or hole in the corporate consciousness.

a. Poetry

A poet often is the prophet of his/her age. T. S. Eliot's poem, "Hollow Men", written in 1925, seems to anticipate the theme of the whole modern epoch. It reads in part:

> We are the hollow men
> We are the stuffed men
> Leaning together
> Headpiece filled with straw. Alas!.[54]

---

[54] T. S. Eliot, "The Hollow Men" (1925) in <u>The Complete Poems and Plays, 1909-1950</u>.

Eliot's image of contemporary man is one who is empty, hollow, vacant, without real substance—appearing normal on the outside, but hollow within. The hollowness, of which Eliot speaks, is a metaphorical way of describing contemporary man's awareness that something is wrong, something vital is missing within the self, leaving a sense of emptiness and meaninglessness. What exactly has been lost? It is difficult to say, but it's as if a sense of wholeness and completeness has been lost, leaving a gaping hole in the inner self.

The American poet, Robert Frost, captured the modern attitude in his poem, "Desert Places":

> They cannot scare me with their empty spaces
> Between stars—on stars where no human race is
> I have it in me so much nearer home
> To scare myself with my own desert places.[55]

b. Sculpture

The artist that best captures the image of the inner void in the human soul is the English sculptor Henry Moore. The theme of the inner void runs through Moore's mammoth bronze and wood sculptures. They are heavy, dense, featureless and nameless figures, often with gaping holes, cavities hollowed out in the torso or head. Moore's pierced and hollow forms remind one of a person through whom a cannon ball had passed. There is solidity, yet emptiness, in Moore's work. The figures are ciphers without identity, faceless effigies that bespeak of No Man and Everyman. As such, they represent Universal Man and Universal Woman. The sculptures are highly stylized and symbolic—sometimes

---

[55] Robert Frost, "Desert Places" (last stanza), <u>Robert Frost, Collected Poems, Prose and Plays</u>, (New York: Literary Classics of the United States, Inc., 1995), p. 269.

barely suggestive of a human form. Consciously or unconsciously, the artist is in contact with the archetypal images from the collective unconscious. They are like Eliot's hollow men searching for a new center, a new core of being and a New Age. Until that new reality arrives, Moore's anonymous figures continue to wait in patient silence. William Barrett comments:

> Moore's faceless hero is everywhere exposed to Nothingness. When, by chance or fate, we fall into an extreme situation, one on the far side of what is normal, routine, accepted, traditional, safeguarded—we are threatened by the void. The solidity of the so-called real world evaporates under the pressure of our situation. Our being reveals itself as much more porous, much less substantial than we had thought it—it is like those cryptic human figures in modern sculpture that are full of holes or gaps.[56]

The concept of a void, or hole, in the human soul is metaphorical language used by the artist to describe his or her perception of the world. When an artist portrays an image of a human with a cavity or hole in the torso, this indicates something is abnormal; something is amiss. The artist's Muse has revealed the emptiness and nothingness that pervades the soul of contemporary humans. Nothingness and hollowness have, in fact, become chief themes in modern art and literature, whether it is directly named or not.

The void is sometimes depicted in other ways, such as the elongated and attenuated figures of the sculptor, Alberto Giacometti. His tall thin images of man bespeak of isolation and alienation. No matter how close one gets to the sculpture, one still feels distant and apart from it. The figures seem to

---

[56]   William Barrett, <u>Irrational Man</u>, p. 60.

be invaded by the surrounding void. How different they are from the classical images of man depicted by the Greek master sculptor Phidias, or the Italian Renaissance sculptor and painter Michelangelo. Their ideal was the well-proportioned, handsome, powerful, god-like figures manifesting perfection in all ways.

c. Painting

One can readily describe the image of man in Greek art or Renaissance art, but when it comes to Modern Art, it is a bit more difficult. According to William Barrett, there is no

> Clear cut image of man amid the bewildering thicket of modern art. The variety of images is too great and too contradictory to coalesce into any single shape or form . . . . A good deal of modern art has been concerned . . . simply with the destruction of the traditional image of man. Man is laid bare, more than that, he is flayed, cut up into bits, and his members strewn everywhere. The human form is often the figure of the faceless and anonymous hero . . . . [57]

The principal work of Expressionist art that depicts the theme of the void is Picasso's <u>Guernica</u>. It is an enormous work representing the bombing of the little Spanish town of Guernica by the Nazis, which occurred on April 18, 1937. The bombing which was at the service of Generalissimo Franco on the open and defenseless Basque city was the initial act of aggression committed against humanity that led to World War II. The painting is an act of rage and protest. It is the most profound protest statement in modern art. It exposes the absurdity of war and the senseless killing

---

[57] <u>Ibid</u>., p. 61.

of innocent lives. About his painting, Picasso said, "No, painting is not interior decoration. It is an instrument of war, for attack and for defense against the enemy." The Guernica is a classic statement of protest against man's inhumanity to man. It used to hang in the New York Museum of Modern Art, but was returned to Spain for the permanent Picasso exhibit there. It embodies dramatic suffering, grief and rage. According to Hans Jaffe,

> In this great painting Picasso created a poignant monument against barbarian aggressive force; though it contains no allusion to the specific event for which it is named, it constitutes a warning to mankind against the implication of unleashing the force of darkness. History proved Picasso right: Warsaw, Rotterdam, Coventry, Smolensk, and Hiroshima are stations along the road which began at Guernica.[58]

And again,

> Picasso expressed his bitter, savage fury over this atrocious deed in an extremely rigorous composition . . . . The austere palette, confined to black, white, and a few shades of gray accentuate the impression of paralyzing terror.[59]

Although the theme of the <u>void in the soul</u> can readily be seen on the faces of the victims in the Guernica, it is also portrayed in the dark, negative spaces on the canvas, which are every bit as important as the positive spaces. Thus the void can be seen in the background where the black expanse surrounds and isolates each figure from the others. That is

---

[58]   Hans L. C. Jaffe, <u>Picasso</u>, p. 37.

[59]   <u>Ibid</u>., p. 39.

the <u>void of nothingness</u>, which engulfs us all. 'That seems to be the main message of the painting. It is one continuous statement, not only of the absurdity of war, but also of life being sucked into the black hole of evil.

Picasso painted a number of works which gave expression to his bitterness at the triumph of injustice. He deforms and distorts the images in response to humanity's own self-debasement through man's inhumanity to man.

Picasso portrays this debased humanity once more in a painting called, "The Weeping Lady", which is detail of the woman portrayed in the larger work, <u>Guernica</u>. What is going on here in the distortion of face and human form in this and other paintings of Picasso? Obviously, he feels free not to duplicate what he sees, but to express what he feels—that <u>things are out of joint</u>!

Another painting that expresses angst and despair before the abyss is that of the Norwegian artist Edvard Munch, a forerunner of the Expressionist movement. The painting titled, <u>The Scream</u>, depicts a sudden moment of apocalyptic revelation that Munch experienced while watching the sunset on a bridge over an Oslo fjord. Most people totally misunderstand Munch's painting. They think that the figure portrayed is the one screaming; however, the existential anguish and terror registered on the face of the lonely figure on the bridge is the result of hearing Nature's primal scream. The figure confronts his destiny—the vast void of nothingness that awaits everyone like a hideous, fire-spitting, cosmic dragon crouching, ready to devour its hapless victim. Munch recounts his experience:

> I was walking down the road with two friends
> when the sun set, suddenly the sky turned as red
> as blood. I stopped and leaned against the fence,
> feeling unspeakably tired. Tongues of fire and
> blood stretched over the bluish black fjord. My
> friends went on walking, while I lagged behind,

shivering with fear. Then I heard the enormous,
infinite scream of nature.[60]

Munch's <u>Scream</u>, like Picasso's <u>Guernica</u>, depicts the artist's feeling of horror and despair over the absurdity of an alien universe which suddenly clashes with human hopes and aspirations. Only when we realize that the tiny little speck of life we call "ourselves" will one day be engulfed by that infinite abyss can we begin to comprehend the absurd vision of the artist. That dark hole is the ultimate fate of all living beings.

When one is brought abruptly to the brink of the abyss, one is confronted with the absurdity and meaninglessness of existence. Paul Tillich describes how this experience has affected modern art. He writes that meaninglessness:

> Is key to the development of visual [art] since the turn of the century. The categories which constitute ordinary experience have lost their power. The category of substance is lost; solid objects are twisted like ropes; the causal interdependence of things is disregarded; things appear in a complete contingency; temporal sequences are without significance, it does not matter whether an event has happened before or after another event; the spatial dimensions are reduced or dissolved into a horrifying infinity. The organic structures of life are cut to pieces which are arbitrarily (from the biological, not the artistic, point of view) recomposed; limbs are dispersed, colors are separated from their natural carriers. The psychological process (this refers to literature more that to art) is reversed; one lives from the future to the past, and this without rhythm or any kind of meaningful

---

[60]   <u>Munch</u>, editor, p. 17.

organization. The world of anxiety is a world in which the categories, the structures of reality, have lost their validity. Everybody would be dizzy if causality suddenly ceased to be valid. In Existential Art . . . causality has lost its validity.[61]

d. The Performing Arts: Drama

The Theater of the Absurd has called into question the traditional cultural values and gives us a new perspective on the encounter with nothingness. It is a challenge to reexamine one's conception of the human condition. It has been said that the image of the <u>Absurd Man</u> is a primary metaphor for our age. The term <u>absurd</u> denotes: devoid of meaning, lacking rational sense. It is akin to the one we have been using to describe the human condition, i.e., the <u>inner void</u>. Both terms indicate the emptiness and hollowness that pervade the human soul.

The playwrights of the Absurd are questioning the easy, superficial answers of our times. Their works are a combination of ridiculous, purposeless behavior and circular talk that gives the plays sometimes a dazzling comic surface. But there is an underlying impression of seriousness and metaphysical distress.

An example of this is Samuel Beckett's play, <u>Waiting for Godot</u>, which does not tell a story; it explores a static situation. Nothing happens, nobody comes, nobody goes, there is just a perpetual waiting. On a country road, by a tree, two old tramps, Vladimir and Estragon, are waiting. That is the opening situation at the beginning of Act I. At the end of Act I, they are informed [by a young boy] that Mr. Godot, with whom they believe they have an appointment, cannot

---

[61]   Paul Tillich, op. Cit., pp. 146-147.

come, but that he will surely come tomorrow. Act I ends in the following manner:

> ESTRAGON: Well, shall we go?
> VLADIMIR: Yes, let's go.
> (They do not move)

In Act II, the play opens the next day, same time, same place. Act II repeats precisely the same pattern as in Act I. The same boy arrives and delivers the same message. After a long, rambling, meaningless dialogue, Estragon says,

> ESTRAGON: I'm tired! (Pause) Let's go.
> VLADIMER: We can't.
> ESTRAGON: Why not?
> VLADIMER: We're waiting for Godot.
> ESTRAGON: Ah! (Pause. Despairing.) What'll
>   we do, what'll we do?
> VLADIMIR: There's nothing we can do.
> ESTRAGON: But we can't go on like this![62]

But it does go on and on, nothing really happens. They just pass the time waiting, and waiting, and waiting . . . for Godot. There are variations in the dialogue between the two acts, but it only serves to emphasize the essential sameness of the situation—the more things change, the more they stay the same. Still Vladimir and Estragon live in hope: they wait for Godot, whose coming will bring the flow of time to a stop. They are hoping to be saved from the evanescence and instability of the illusion of time, and to find peace and permanence outside it. Then they will no longer be tramps, homeless wanderers, but will have arrived home.

---

[62] Samuel Beckett, <u>Waiting for Godot</u>.

According to Martin Esslin in his book, <u>The Theater of the Absurd</u>,

> It has been suggested that Godot is a weakened form of "God", a dimunitive form, but there is no indication from the author that either is so . . . whether Godot is meant to suggest the intervention of a supernatural agency, or whether he stands for a mythical human being whose arrival is expected to change this situation . . . its exact nature is of secondary importance. The subject of the play is not Godot but waiting, an act of waiting as an essential and characteristic aspect of the human condition. Throughout our lives we always wait for something, and Godot simply represents the objective of our waiting— an event, a thing, a person, death.[63]

In this drama, the <u>void in the human soul</u> is represented by the emptiness, hollowness and meaninglessness in the lives of those who ultimately have no hope.

e. Performing Arts: Music

The atonality and percussive dissonance of Expressionist music corresponds to the anti-rationalism of the times. It, like the Theater of the Absurd, rejects the traditional forms of the past. What it seeks to express in musical form is the absurdity of existence. It is interesting to note that the word <u>absurd</u> comes from the two Latin words: <u>ab</u>—from, and <u>surdus</u>— deaf, i.e., "to be tone deaf." Atonality and dissonance affect humans at the deepest level of their sensibility. It strikes them

---

[63]   Martin Esslin, <u>The Theater of the Absurd</u>.

that something is "out of tune" and disharmonious. That is exactly what absurdity is, not just in music, but in all life.

With the turn of the century, nineteenth century Romanticism in music, like the Impressionistic style in art, gave way to the modern form analogous to the Expressionistic movement in art. One authority describes the new emphasis in music:

> The experimental works of Arnold Schoenberg and Igor Stravinsky about 1910 heralded a new epoch in music. Schoenberg was the pioneer when his adoption of the ideals of the Expressionist movement—like Impressionism; an aesthetic development shared by other art forms—resulted in his discarding traditional concepts of consonance and dissonance as well as tonality and led into the development of atonality . . . Stravinsky's revolutionary style . . . concentrated on metric imbalance and percussive dissonance and introduced a decade of extreme experimentation that coincided with World War I, period of major social and political upheaval.[64]

Thus for modern music, gone are the Romantic melodies and harmonies of the 19th century; in its place are the disharmonies and dissonances of the 20th and 21st centuries. The theme of a "hole in Being" would be found primarily in the dark mood that it expressed.

2. Literature

If the writer's task is to reflect the image of man embedded in the culture of his or her own time, what is

---

[64] Encyclopedia Britannic (Macro ed., 1985), vol. 12, p. 714.

the predominant image of man in contemporary culture? The answer to that daunting question comes not from an arbitrary decision. The image of man is shaped by our contemporary worldview, which in turn is determined by the cosmology of the age. Modern cosmology, with its attendant presuppositions, is a given; not a matter of choice.

Post-Copernican cosmology has had profound consequences for the image of man. Mankind is no longer a special, divine creation in a closed world under a vast celestial dome. He is only one animal among millions on a vast cosmic stage of infinite proportions. Everything about the human reality, along with the universe, has been relativized. There are no longer any absolutes to cling to for security or to guide one's course of action. Modern humans are suddenly alone in a vast and indifferent universe.

In response to this radical change in cosmology and its consequent world view, the modern writer has been forced to rethink and retool his craft to reflect those changes. Old images and forms no longer suffice; they do not communicate to a rootless and relativized age.

The writer is faced with the human predicament of addressing people with infinite aspirations in an absurd universe. If the writer undertakes to say anything significant about human reality, he or she must take into account the modern worldview and its image of man. Human aspirations find no validation in an icy, indifferent universe without purpose or meaning.

In light of this, the writer is forced to reask the most fundamental of all questions: Who is man? What is his role in this vast enterprise called life? And, by what values should he live? The bedrock reality for humans and the standard by which it is to be measured is no longer the hero of John Milton's <u>Paradise Lost</u>; rather, it more closely resembles the antihero of Albert Camus, Franz Kafka, Fyodor Dostoievsky and James Joyce.

Albert Camus' favorite antihero was the Greek mythological character, Sisyphus. As the result of his actions,

Sisyphus offended the gods; therefore, he was condemned to the everlasting punishment of rolling a huge rock up to the top of the mountain, only to have it roll back down into the valley below. Each time this occurred, Sisyphus was required to descend the mountain and repeat the task all over again throughout all eternity. Truly, if any situation could be characterized as absurd, this is it. Sisyphus could neither finish his task, nor point to any lasting accomplishment. For Camus, Sisyphus was the Absurd Hero. He typified the life of so many modern humans who go through life performing the daily grind just to make ends meet, with little or no hope of improving their lot. Camus wrote of the plight of millions:

> Rising, streetcar, four hours in the office or the factory, meal, streetcar, four hours of work, meal, sleep, and Monday Tuesday Wednesday Thursday Friday and Saturday according to the same rhythm . . . . [65]

This is the daily round of existence for so many. But one day, it occurs to the individual to ask, Why? Why am I locked into this futile existence like a caged gerbil running on an exercise wheel? Why am I living like this? What is life all about anyway? Then the true absurdity of existence dawns upon the individual. This kind of existence is going nowhere. It is <u>absurd</u>!

Franz Kafka is another modern author who wrote eloquently about the absurd. In his work entitled, <u>The Trial</u>[66] he narrates how "K" an unsuspecting citizen is summoned before the Court to stand trial; however, he was never read an indictment of the charges. He was instructed to see an attorney and prepare for trial. As the story unfolds, Kafka

---

[65]   Albert Camus, <u>The Myth of Sisyphus</u> (New York: Vintage, 1955), p. 10.

[66]   Franz Kafka, <u>The Trial</u>, (New York: Knopf, translated 1956 by Walla and Edwin Miller).

describes with great skill the frustration of trying to deal with the intricacies of a cumbersome, bloated, impersonal, rule-bound, incomprehensible legal bureaucracy. Despite endless attempts to find out the charges and the crime for which he had been accused, he was never successful. He went from attorney to attorney, clerk to administrator, magistrate to judge, and back again, without ever finding satisfaction. Finally, sentence was passed and he was led out by two officers of the court and assassinated without ever discovering his crime. A truly absurd situation.

A similar tale is recounted by Kafka in <u>The Castle</u>, only the antihero is an architect who was summoned to the castle of the village to carry out a project on behalf of the lord or the castle; however, he was never able to gain admission to the castle because the gatekeeper had to obtain clearance first, which never seemed to be forthcoming. Again, it is a parable about the frustrations of dealing with an absurd, mindless, impersonal bureaucracy and the inability to break through all of the red tape.

Perhaps, the best illustration of Kafka's skill in presenting the absurdity of life was in his short story called, <u>The Metamorphosis</u>. It is about an employee in a large corporate firm who woke up one morning to find that he had been transformed over night into a huge, disgusting cockroach-like insect. And if that weren't enough, he was on his back in bed unable to turn over and get out of bed because his tiny legs could only paw the air and wouldn't enable him to resolve his predicament. He could neither get up and go to work, nor perform his job-related tasks if he could. He wasn't able to inform his employer that he wouldn't be coming to work; but even if he could, he would be too embarrassed and ashamed to admit what had happened to him. His predicament was both tragic and absurd.

<u>Metamorphosis</u> is a study of dehumanization and depersonalization in the technological age. Persons have been turned into nameless ciphers who are helpless to alter their

destiny. This results in a condition of no longer being valued as a human being; instead, persons have been reduced to thinghood. This causes a sense of shame, worthlessness, loss of self-esteem, and self-hatred. One is put in the double-bind of being dehumanized, yet unable to affect a change. A sense of the absurdity of such a life creeps into one's consciousness, which only exacerbates the problem even more. Kafka's essay is a protest against all such dehumanization of mass society in the Technological Age. It is like Joseph Heller's antihero in <u>Catch 22</u>, where one is placed in an absurd situation, yet there is little opportunity to determine one's destiny—that's the catch!

The third author that shall be used to illustrate the theme of the absurd in contemporary literature is William Faulkner. Faulkner caught the spirit of the absurdist movement in his 1929 novel, <u>The Sound and the Fury</u>.[67] Faulkner's book is a "stream of consciousness" novel in that without introduction or explanation, it plunges the reader into the ongoing dialogue between the Comptons, a poor white Mississippi family and their shiftless slaves (Faulkner's term). The Comptons typify the Post-Civil War plantation farmers who had lost their former Southern life-style and who tried to eke out a living on what was left of their former land holdings.

The dialogue begins by exposing the reader to the petty biases, trivia, and mundane concerns of these largely ignorant people who are only one step above those they refer to as "poor white trash." Initially, the dialogue, as narrated, is told from the perspective of the 33 year-old family moron named "Benjy" (Benjamin Compton). Although Faulkner never mentions it, and the reader might miss it on first reading, the fact that the narration reflects the viewpoint of the family idiot, underscores the theme of the novel taken from Shakespeare's <u>Macbeth</u>, "Life is a tale <u>told by an idiot</u>."

---

[67]   William Faulkner, <u>The Sound and Fury</u>. (New York: Random House, 1951).

The narration begins in a flat two-dimensional style with no depth. Time shifts occur like flashbacks, yet there is no indication in the narrative that this is the case, except for the fact that the text is set off in italics. It represents the mental processes of the family idiot where life has little or no context or perspective. Things just flow together without a temporal framework.

The story plods endlessly on describing the misery and triviality of their daily lives, yet the drama never seems to get anywhere. Indeed, the novel simply ends without climax or denoucment. Nothing gets resolved. Their lives seem to have no purpose or meaning.

Faulkner has deliberately crafted his novel to emphasize the quote from Shakespeare's <u>Macbeth</u>:

> Out, out, brief candle!
> Life's but a walking shadow, a poor player,
> That struts and frets his hour upon the stage
> And then is heard no more. <u>It is a tale</u>
> <u>Told by an idiot, full of sound and fury,</u>
> <u>Signifying nothing!</u> (emphasis added)[68]

The novel is both a metaphorical statement and a global indictment of all human doings. Life goes on endlessly, but in the final analysis, it has no purpose or goal. It is going nowhere and accomplishes nothing. This establishes Faulkner firmly within the absurdist tradition. There is no ultimate meaning or value in human doings—they just are.

3. Philosophy

Philosophy is the human attempt to comprehend the universe by discerning a rational coherence and order within

---

[68]   Shakespeare, <u>Macbeth</u>, Act V, Sc. V, ln. 19.

all of its complexity, multiplicity and diversity. That task has become extremely urgent in our contemporary Postmodern World, where philosophy is faced with "the yawning void of relativism left by modernity's dissolution of traditional world views."[69]

Over the sweep of the last 2,500 years, the Western Mind has built many mansions of meaning in which the human spirit has found a home. These philosophies, or dwellings of the soul, have served their purpose in the age for which they were constructed. The great systematizers of thought such as: Plato, Aristotle, Plotinus, Augustine, Aquinas, Descartes, Kant and Hegel were able to bring together all of the diverse elements of their culture and express them in great <u>summas</u> of thought that remained persuasive for generations thereafter. However, each has come and gone. They have had their day and served their purpose; but the human mind has moved on. Each age comes to the table with a new set of questions and concerns.

In wake of the Copernican Revolution and the ensuing Enlightenment, the human being was displaced from a position of central importance to a relative peripheral position in a vast and impersonal universe. The result, according to Tarnas, was that "Modern Man now increasingly sensed his alienation from nature's womb . . . [and] his confinement to an absurd universe . . . devoid of meaning."[70]

It is this context that the existential philosophy of Jean-Paul Sartre must be assessed. In his brilliant dialectical <u>tour de force</u> entitled, <u>Being and Nothingness</u>, Sartre sets forth his views on human existence. The title of his book provides a clue as to his approach. It is the age-old problem of being and becoming, but with a new twist. How can the stability of being, as described by Parmenides, include the dynamism of change and transformation? The answer to that puzzle,

---

[69]   Tarnas, op.cit., p. 412.
[70]   <u>Ibid., p. 376.</u>

according to Sartre, lies in the unique power of the human mind to create nothingness. This takes place in the dialectical process of questioning.

Man is the being who questions. He is that being who interrogates being. He asks what does it mean to be? There is a fundamental distinction between man and what he questions. In order to emphasize that distinction, Sartre calls man a being "for-itself," whereas, the impersonal world and all that it contains is called "in-itself." On the one hand, the in-itself is inert, substantial and unchanging. It just is! On the other hand, human reality, or the for-itself, is personal, free, and constantly changing.

> Sartre's use of the reflexive pronoun "for-itself" derives from Hegelian terminology and it contributes to a certain confusion when speaking of the personal. It needs to be understood and employed with that caution in mind. He could have used the reflexive term "for-myself," but that would have been too individualistic and not general enough for an ontology.

Man, the for-itself, is characterized by the notions of lack, desire and possibility. Humans experience themselves as lack, something incomplete. This becomes apparent in one's projects and desires which are projected before oneself as what one hopes to accomplish; and therefore, what one hopes to become. Desire exposes the lack of being; therefore, humans are the desire to be. He/she is always characterized as possibility, never static, always open to change.

The for-itself, however, feels uneasy with this openedness and seeks to establish itself in permanence, like the in-itself; but, that would be bad faith—the attempt to be that which it is not. This constant desire to be self-founding, to overcome lack and become complete is the desire to become Being-itself, i.e., "God." Man's desire to be God is impossible, says Sartre, because God does not exist; consequently, man is called the "impossible possibility."

In essence, Sartre's analysis of man as lack is what this study has called: <u>the being with an inner void</u>. One is constantly seeking to overcome that lack, to fill that void, to become whole and complete. One questions that which is, in order to open up new possibilities of what might be. This annihilating of the of the "isness" of being creates a gap of nothingness in the mental process that must be bridged if discursive thought is to flow in a continuous logical sequence. Rational thought requires that these gaps of nothingness be filled. This dialectic lies at the root of the creative process and without it the advances of human culture would not be possible.

Sartre calls this ability of the human mind to create nothingness the "worm hole in being." Sartre employs the figurative image of "mind worms", or tiny questions that eat away at Being creating holes or gaps of nothingness in the smooth consistency of Being. That image is apt because it indicates that the power to question, which is the source of human creativity, also has its downside. It highlights the dual nature of questioning not only to create, but also to destroy. Just as the tiny crawling animal called a worm eats away at the core of an apple leaving a hole at the heart of the fruit; so likewise, the little question eats away at the great systems of thought by calling them into question and gradually destroying them from the inside out.

If one might be permitted to change Sartre's metaphor from <u>worms and apples</u> to <u>termites and houses,</u> then one has an insect that feeds upon wood fiber rather than fruit. When the termite gains entry to the wood framework of a home, it continues to bore in silently, but steadily, and eats away at the structure so that the wooden supports become honeycombed with holes, until at last, it becomes like so much Swiss cheese. Eventually, if left unchecked, the structure becomes so weakened that the walls begin to fall away, the roof comes down, and the whole building collapses.

In similar manner, the insignificant little question silently and relentlessly chews away at the foundations of the great systems of thought until gradually, bite by bite, the whole structure becomes so weakened that it too collapses. Such is the destructive power and ruinous effect of the tiny question. It eats away at the structure of meaning that humans have so carefully fashioned until the structure falls like a house of cards. The little question can bring down the tallest towers of meaning that have been constructed to house the human spirit. That, historically, has been the fate of all the great compendiums of intellectual thought by the human race. Each was constructed as a permanent abode for the human spirit in order to make life more tolerable; but, over time, each was destroyed, not from without by the wrecker's ball; but rather, from within by the erosive forces of modernity. Consequently, all of those magnificent structures of meaning have fallen, leaving humans once more exposed to the naked void of total relativity and an existence without foundation or purpose.

Probably, the single most important event of the 21st century has been the terrorist attack on the Twin Towers of the International Trade Center in New York City. They symbolized the grandeur and pride of Technological Man with his awesome ability to construct towers reaching to the sky. But as everyone knows, in the year of 2001 on that fateful day of 9/11, those magnificent skyscrapers came crashing down into a monumental pile of dust and smoldering rubble. The termites of hatred razed those Twin Towers.

These are metaphors for our time—not just for the American people, but for the entire world. Although it may not be as dramatic in its ability to capture headlines, the collapse of the Towers of Meaning from the past has resulted in the Postmodern Age of relativism. It has left the Western

Mind's skyscrapers of meaning in shambles. The termites of doubt and cynicism have so eroded the confidence in the ability of the Western Mind that it can no longer offer a secure home in which to live. There are no longer any over-arching systems of meaning to bind society together. The crisis in philosophy parallels that of the arts and literature. Intellectual forces have combined to dissolve the unifying glue of society.

A question can create or destroy. Like a hammer, it is a tool that can shape or smash, create or crush. There is a certain ambivalence to the power of critical questioning. The little question, which seemingly is so innocuous, has the power to build or bring down those dwelling places of the human spirit in which we live and move and have our being.

The problem of emptiness and meaninglessness in the human heart is engendered by the power to question. The questioning ability makes one aware of the contradiction between the impersonal, soulless, physical universe and the purposive aspirations of the human soul. Through questioning, humans realize that they are strangers and aliens in a hostile environment; otherwise, they would be like the rest of the animal kingdom, totally unaware of their destiny and of the spiritual vacuum that humans experience, i.e., the metaphorical "hole", or void, in the human soul. Humans have the feeling that they have lost their center, that there is a vast gulf, a cavern, within the soul that results in <u>enui</u>, listlessness and estrangement. There is a dissonance in the human soul, a feeling that it is out of harmony with its Source—the vast impersonal universe.

That, in conclusion, is the unanimous testimony of modern art—both visual and performing—and likewise, with contemporary literature and existential philosophy. It constitutes the crisis of our time. How does one come to terms with the void that is so pervasive and all-consuming? Answering that query is the burden of this analysis of the inner void.

Chapter IX

THE GRANDEUR AND MISERY OF MAN

We have observed how extensive is the theme of voidness in the arts, literature and philosophy. Something that basic must spring from something elemental in the human makeup. This study proposes that the sense of voidness in the inner self derives in part from the way humans think and process their perceptions of the world. How this works will become apparent when one examines how the mind functions in its dialectic of inquiry, which is the topic of this chapter.

1. The Grandeur

Homo sapiens is the most advanced of all species in the animal kingdom. Charles Darwin called man "the wonder and glory of the universe."[71] William Shakespeare heaped paeans of praise upon Man as the noblest of all creatures. His Hamlet proclaimed:

> What a piece of work is man! How noble in
> reason! How infinite in faculty! In form and

---

[71]   Charles Darwin, <u>The Descent of Man</u>, ch. 6.

> moving how express and admirable! In action
> how like an angel! In apprehension how like
> a god! The beauty of the world! The paragon
> of animals! And yet, to me, what is this
> quintessence of dust?[72]

Truly, the human animal is endowed with powers that enable it to out perform and far surpass the rest of the animal kingdom.

From the anthropologist's perspective, humans are superior because of certain physiological features. Man is a warm-blooded mammal with upright posture. This enabled him to become bipedal, freeing his hands for tasks other than locomotion. The development of the opposable thumb allowed primitive man to become a tool-maker and perform countless other tasks. By evolving a face with frontal eyes, it gave him binocular vision thus permitting him the ability to judge distances better and to focus on prey or foe.

Those physical features, important as they were in the development of man, are not to be compared with his most important trait of all—the development of his <u>mental</u> capacities, especially his linguistic ability. With the development of the throat to process language, there came with speech a host of other powers such as reasoning, the power to question, self-transcendence, self-awareness and freedom to choose. Imagination and creativity also became crucial as man's conceptual powers evolved. All of these powers combined to make the human brain the most complex and versatile organism in the known universe.

Among all these acquired mental traits, the one that probably has changed human destiny the most is the power to question. That power will be examined in some detail, since it is key to understanding how the human mind is able to conceive of the outer and inner voids, which are the chief

---

[72]   Shakespeare, <u>Hamlet</u>, Act II, Sc. ii, lns. 319-323.

concerns of this study. An extensive analysis of this awesome power has been given in my book, <u>The Spiral of Inquiry</u>. If I might be permitted to quote from that work,

> The power to question is that ability of the inquiring mind to move from its primary perceptions and sensory impressions to the level of reflection and intelligence. It means that capacity of the critical mind to challenge, weigh and evaluate the raw data in such a way that one can fit it together into a meaningful whole.[73]

Perception, by its very nature, requires a judgment by the observer, and to make any judgment is to decide between two alternatives. For example, the eye receives a visual image; then, it fires off signals to the cerebral cortex, which forms a symbolic image. The brain must then decide what these images mean. The mind is faced with the questions: What is it? What does it mean? Is it something familiar, or alien? The mind must interpret the data and decide between the alternatives, which means answering the questions put to it.

This ability to question is a universal experience for humankind. Furthermore, it is a fundamental structure for all human experience. The very possibility of having experience is dependent upon this underlying structure of human understanding, i.e., the dialectic of question and answer.

In true Kantian form, the power to question is that interpretive apparatus by which the mind processes sensory impressions and primary perceptions of the empirical world and structures them into meaningful, rational concepts. Thus it is the means whereby humans acquire knowledge.

There is probably no experience more universal to humankind than the ability to question. It goes to the very

---

[73]   A. Harms, <u>The Spiral of Inquiry</u>, (Delaware: University Press of America, 1999), p. 37.

heart and essence of our humanity. It is the presupposition for all human thinking. It is the power that sets humans apart from the other animals and enables homo sapiens to become the dominant animal on the planet.

The potential of this power is awesome. In questioning lies the power to take humankind anywhere, do anything, conquer any foe, or explore the unknown—it even permits humans to embark on space travel to the moon, the planets and beyond. Virtually nothing is beyond human reach. The probative power of a question can penetrate the darkest mystery, solve the most enigmatic puzzle, and disclose the deepest secrets.

Given the importance of this aptitude, what must be presupposed about humankind? First and foremost is the rational component. "Man is a reasoning animal," wrote the Roman philosopher Seneca. The ability to question involves the capacity to think logically and rationally. Questioning and reasoning are so intertwined that it is difficult to dissociate them. The human ability to think analytically and critically depends upon the ability to question; and questioning depends upon the logical ability to distinguish between identity and difference. A question arises when some difference is observed and the mind asks, Why?

Questioning lies as the root of thinking itself. In fact, persons think by question-and-answer. What we call "thinking" is the dialectical process wherein the mind inquires into something by posing a question to itself; it then systematically seeks an answer. When it arrives at a plausible answer, a judgment is passed on it, either accepting it or rejecting it. After arriving at a tentative answer on any particular matter, the mind asks additional questions, which in turn provides the basis for further questions and a clarification of the initial answer. In this manner, the mind advances step-by-step in a process whereby it is led to an ever closer approximation of the truth.

All thinking involves this dialectical process. It is called discursive reasoning because an inner dialogue takes place, a discourse, whereby the mind by a process of Q and A enables humans to build up a body of tested and reliable knowledge.

Thus the human ability to question depends upon the capacity to think logically. When the mind detects some inconsistency or contradiction in the logic of the situation, the matter becomes questionable. When one speaks of the logic of the situation, one refers to the principles of thinking, such as the law of the excluded middle, sometimes called the law of noncontradiction: an entity cannot both be and not be at the same time.

When an inconsistency arises, the mind sends up a signal that something has gone awry in the smooth, logical continuity of the rational processes, and that precipitates a question. A disjunction in the reasoning process is recognized by the mind as a discontinuity, or gap in the thinking process, and this precipitates a question. The question is a request that the gap be filled. Indeed, the gap must be filled if one's thinking is not to be plagued with non sequiturs and illogical conclusions. The dynamic of gap-filling in one's rational thinking process is a primal pattern that gets reflected in all human activities, including work and play.

In sports, the goal is usually to put a ball into a hole, e.g., golf, basketball, billiards, skeeball, etc. The hole may be round or symbolized in other shapes such as the netted goal of ice hockey and soccer, or perhaps the goalposts in the game of football. It may be a bull's eye on a target, but the idea is essentially the same—to put the projectile, whether bullet, arrow or dart—within the target circle, preferably the bull's eye.

In a different context, the hole may be symbolized by a blank canvas on the artist's easel, which calls out to be filled with images of beauty or meaning. The same would be true of a blank wall upon which a mural is painted; or, for baser types, a subway wall to be filled with graffiti. People seem to be impelled to fill blank spaces with something—anything that comes to mind if it entertains or informs. People won't pay to sit in a theater and stare at a blank screen; but, when that blank screen, through the magic of movies, gets filled with images, it becomes a window through which one views the lives of fascinating persons and stirring events—both past and present.

The same fundamental idea is true in one's vocation. For the mathematician, the blank is the unknown "x" in his equations, which requires to be filled with a rational answer. For the writer, it is a blank page that must be filled. The author must transform an empty sheet into scintillating prose and well-connected thoughts. Business persons seek to fill their daytimers with productive appointments and activities. The song writer seeks to fill the airways with the sound of his or her music. We all seek to fill our time with useful projects and interests.

The same pattern is even found to be true in sexual relations. The male seeks to fill the vagina with his manhood; and the female seeks to be filled. One might note that the terminology of the electrician or plumber reflects the same notion with the "male" and "female" connections for plugs and pipes.

The same idea holds true of one's dining habits. There one is constantly seeking to fill one's "pie-hole" with food. In that case, the "vast void within" is the empty stomach; however, for the obese, it is not physical hunger, but an emotional void that causes one to overeat.

The human mind has even found it difficult to imagine empty space, and for most of history has wanted to fill space with an invisible material called <u>ether</u>—that is, until Albert Michelson and Edward Morely performed an experiment in 1887 that proved no such material existed—which left only the abysmal void.

There is something within the human heart that hates a void. It is like the old adage: "Nature hates a vacuum."

Likewise, the inner void <u>must</u> be filled with meaning. Each person seeks a life full of joy and happiness—whether in work or play, in sex or dining. All human activity exhibits the primordial drive to fill the void within one's life.

The power to question is mankind's discovery power, and as such, it is one of the basic human aptitudes. It involves the ability to probe the unknown, discover what is new, and to disclose the truth. It is that probative, creative ability that enables humans to suspend present belief and to create new possibilities. It lies at the basis of every creative act. The capacity of the mind to create gaps of nothingness, or blanks, that need to be filled, is the source of all human creativity. The mind has the power to annihilate, i.e., to create nothingness; and then, seek to fill that void. For example, the mind plays games of "what if." It poses a hypothesis: if "y" is assigned a certain value, then what would be "x"? the "x" becomes the unknown in the mental equation that needs to be filled with a meaningful, rational answer. By this process of creating nothingness, or gaps, that which is creatively new can emerge.

The process of gap-filling is at the root of all learning. John Dewey used the analogy of a traveler who comes to a deep ditch blocking him from his designated destination. An enterprising traveler will fashion a crude bridge made of logs or some other material; and then, cross over so that he can finish his journey. Likewise, the mind comes across an inconsistency or break in the logic of the situation; and then, it creatively fashions a mental bridge over the gap. By this process of gap-filling, the mind gradually constructs an integrated, consistent body of knowledge.

All the great libraries of the world, the most advanced technological inventions, the magnificent, soaring, skyscrapers, the space missions to the moon and other planets, all owe their success to this unique and amazing power to question. It is the source of every academic discipline—whether it be science, history, literature, etc. The advances of human culture are the result of accumulated knowledge over the centuries built up brick-by-brick, question-by-question, until it seems that there is virtually nothing that humans cannot accomplish.

Shakespeare's praise of mankind calling man the noblest of all creatures in <u>Hamlet</u>, cannot be considered too lavish. The psalmist in the Hebrew Bible says of man: "What is man that you are mindful of him . . . For you have made him a little lower than the gods."[74]

This theme was picked up by Pico della Mirandola during the beginning of the Renaissance in his celebrated <u>Oration on the Dignity of Man</u>. It was Pico who described the high status of mankind, even to partaking in the divine,

> O Adam . . . you are confined to no limits, shall determine for yourself your own nature, in accordance with your own free will . . . . We have made you neither heavenly nor earthly, neither mortal nor immortal, so that, more freely and more honorably the molder and maker of yourself, you may fashion yourself in whatever form you shall prefer. You shall be able to descend among the lower forms of being, which are the brute beasts; you shall be able to be reborn out of the judgment of your own soil into the higher beings, which are divine.[75]

According to Pico, man has the ability to be and do whatever he chooses, even to ascending to union with the

---

[74]   Psalm 8:4,5. Some translators shy away from the original Hebrew word for "gods" and translate it as "angels"; but the true words of the psalmist give a much higher status for man than the angels; see also Psalm 82:6.

[75]   Pico della Mirandola, <u>Oratory on the Dignity of Man</u>, quoted in Tarnas, op. cit. pp. 214-215.

divine. Truly, the dignity of mankind meant something special both to the psalmist and Pico, as well as other humanists of the Renaissance.

The Grandeur of Man, we have argued, results from his questioning power. Since questioning is the marvelous power that makes humans stand apart from the rest of the animal kingdom, mankind can be defined as <u>animal interrogans</u>, the Inquiring Animal. Mankind's grandeur lies in this unique power that enables it to challenge the status quo, to innovate, to change course, to create a culture, to excel beyond all other beings on earth. By this power, mankind can conceive of the infinite, the eternal.

Armed with this awesome new mental tool, humans began to move beyond mundane questions about food and shelter to questions about the universe: What is meant by infinite space? What is an infinite series? Was there a First Cause? What is meant by eternity, unlimited time? Have things always been so? What is the destiny of mankind? What is Ultimate Reality, the Totality, the All-encompassing? What is meant by the Void—both outer and inner?

Soren Kierkegaard, the forerunner of existential philosophy, gave expression to some of these concerns:

> What is this great enterprise called life? Why am I a part of it and how did I get here? What is its meaning? If I am expected to take part in it, what is expected of me? Why was I not consulted? Who is in charge? I would like to have a word with him.[76]

Questions like these plagued the minds of men and gave rise to philosophy and the religious quest. The power of humans to inquire, to ask searching questions

---

[76]   Soren Kierkegaard, <u>Fear and Trembling</u>, p. 101.

about themselves and the cosmos, became the defining characteristic of human beings.

2. The Misery

Ironically, the human malaise, or what we have called the misery of man, stems from that which is the cause or his grandeur. The nobility that the human being has earned as the Inquiring Animal, the creator of culture, is also the source of his downfall.

Mankind's power to question is driven by what I have termed the "interrogative gene."[77] The interrogative gene is the engine that drives the inquirer forward in a dialectical progression so that when one answer is found to a question, additional questions are raised, and so on, ad infinitum. The inquirer is always kept off balance because his questions always exceed his answers. This unlimited power to question, with all of its magnificent potential, results in man's biggest problem—his questions never come to an end. Consequently, he is relentlessly impelled to solve the next problem, to accomplish the next project, to master the next body of knowledge, and so, on and on.

In short, man is condemned to a permanent restlessness that will never bring peace to his heart or a sense of finality to his incessant questioning. Therefore, he is sentenced to be unfulfilled and eternally dissatisfied with the present state of things.

---

[77] The unique powers of the human brain are hard-wired into the genetic code of the human being's DNA molecule. This would include the power of language and the dialectic process of question-and-answer, which is so closely tied to rational thought. The "interrogative gene" is postulated as the anticipated result of future human genome research.

Some see only good in that restlessness, saying that it is the source of human creativity and grandeur. Yet, that drive to excel and to surpass all prior accomplishments has its downside. It leads to unbridled ambition that can only result in eventual disappointment and disillusionment. It is more than a cliché to say, "Man's reach always exceeds his grasp."

In matters of pleasure-seeking, wealth-accumulation, fame, adulation and power, there is never enough. Greed drives the market place. Envy and desire, not only to "keep up with the Joneses," but to surpass them, has been the downfall of many a household. One is in perpetual competition with others to outdo and surpass them in personal esteem and community acceptance.

In matters of money, the goal is to be listed in the top 100 wealthiest persons. In business, it is to be the head of a "Fortune 500" company. Humans are continually ranking one another and seeking to be numero uno, e.g., as the CEO of a GE, an IBM, a Microsoft; or they seek to become "Man of the Year" on the cover of Time magazine, an MVP in sports, a Nobel Prize winner in research, President, Chief-of-Staff, an Oscar winner in the film industry, or to be listed in Who's Who? In religion, it is the attitude of "I'm holier that thou"; and in the world of philanthropy, it is, "I'm more generous than thou."

One might well ask, what is wrong with that? Perhaps, nothing, except that human desires are insatiable. The individual seeks unlimited knowledge, fame, power, wealth, praise and adulation. The problem is, nothing finite can satisfy the inquiring mind. No matter how rich a person may be s/he always wants more. As the sage observed, "[T]he eyes of man are never satisfied."[78]

According to Jean-Paul Sartre, what one really desires is to be omnipotent, omniscient, infinite and absolute—in other words, to be "God." For some, even that is not enough.

---

[78] Proverbs 27:20b

The Mexican General Antonio Lopez de Santa Anna is reported to have said, "If I were to be God, I would wish for more."[79] Since being God is impossible, Sartre calls man an "impossible possibility." Human passions can never be satisfied; therefore, Sartre writes, humans are a "useless passion." They are condemned to a life of restlessness, dissatisfaction, disillusionment, frustration, and finally, despair. It was said of Alexander the Great that, after he had conquered the whole world, he sat down and wept because there were no more worlds to conquer. The desires of humankind are insatiable; hence, humans are condemned to be everlastingly dissatisfied and unfulfilled. The source of humanity's grandeur is also the source of his misery.

There is another resolution of the age-old problem of humankind, and that is found in Buddhism. For Gautama, the historical Buddha, the problem is more fundamental. It is in desire itself; but that will be treated later under the topic of **Religious Answers.**

---

[79]   A quote from the President-General of Mexico, Antonio Lopez de Santa Anna, from an article by Bronson Tate in the <u>Smithsonian</u> periodical, April 2002.

Chapter X

SIZING THE INNER VOID

The central question that has only been alluded to so far must now be addressed: What do humans seek? What do they require for a sense of completeness and fulfillment? In broad general terms, one can say that the quest for wholeness and fulfillment is at bottom the search for that which brings happiness. The British historian H. G. Wells suggested that what all humans seek is happiness;[80] but that only leads to a further question: What brings happiness? One is still left with the underlying question of what brings contentment and wholeness to the self?

Any attempt to assess the extent of the human need involves scaling the size of the inner void, which is no small task. It's like being asked to describe the limits of desire. What is the difference between desire in general and that which is needed to fill the inner void? What are the wants and needs required for a happy life? It is difficult to measure something so subjective; but that distinction must be drawn in order properly to define the extent of the void within.

The sense of voidness in the human species probably does not stem from the absence of any one thing; rather, it results from a combination of factors—all of which are necessary for humans to feel complete and whole. Humans are complex animals. Their requirements for satisfaction are manifold in

---

[80]   H. G. Wells, <u>Outline of History</u>, Chap. 40, p.

accordance with their multi-faceted nature. Aspects of the human psyche that must be considered include, but are not limited to, the following seven categories: physico-mental, emotional, intellectual, aesthetic, spiritual, psycho-social and volitional.

An essential component in one's personal makeup involves, first, good <u>physical and mental health</u>. Body and mind are inescapably intertwined, as psychosomatic medicine has demonstrated. A debilitating physical disease can cause mental depression, and vice versa. Good mental health is directly related to a stable environment where one's basic needs of sustenance, shelter and security are met. They are basic to holistic health. If both physical and psychological needs are not met, the human soul develops a sense of deprivation and loss.

A second vital component of personhood is to have the full spectrum of <u>emotional needs</u> expressed and validated. Everyone desires to be loved and accepted by one's peers. A feeling of worth and self-esteem is essential to human health and happiness. Enthusiasm and excitement about life—that <u>elan vitale</u> which gives life its spark and zest—is indispensable for a full and happy life. Likewise, humor and comedy relief can bring perspective and balance to life. "Laughter is the best medicine," it is said. Everyone needs an emotional outlet. Without that, life becomes dull, drab, monotonous and boring, resulting in the feeling that something vital and necessary is missing.

The third essential facet of life is the <u>intellectual component</u>. With it comes an active curiosity and sense of wonder about life. Aristotle wrote, "All men by nature want to know."[81] They want to learn, grow and actualize their potential. A large interior life fueled by an inquiring mind is one of the greatest joys of life. As Richard Tarnas writes:

> The direct apprehension of the world's deeper
> reality satisfies not only the mind but the soul;

---

[81]   Aristotle, <u>Metaphysics</u>, Bk. I, Chap. 1.

> it is in essence, a redemptive vision, a sustaining insight into the true nature of things that is at once intellectually decisive and spiritually liberating.[82]

The rational component in the human makeup has led philosophers and scientists to seek the timeless order that lies behind the chaos and flux of phenomena. It has led to the creativity and imagination that has fueled human culture and progress. Without an active intellectual life, an individual is deprived of one of life's greatest rewards.

For many, the fourth category of <u>aesthetic sensibility</u> kindled by the love of beauty, symmetry and harmony is paramount to a fulfilled life. Being touched by one's Muse brings, as Plato wrote, "a divine madness," an inspiration and ebullience that transports the artist or poet into a state of ecstasy. Here intellectual, emotional and spiritual dimensions all combine into one. That which is most important to the innermost soul can only be expressed in the symbolic language of myth, metaphor and music. The poetry of the soul requires that the ineffable be expressed in a language inaccessible to a rigid, rational and logical vocabulary. Here one encounters the depths of the unconscious, the hidden cauldron of emotion in the soul. Surely, human existence would be greatly depleted of vitality without the aesthetic expression.

All of these personality components that have been mentioned are active in the fifth, or <u>spiritual dimension</u> of life; yet the spiritual is not limited to any one, or combination of, the above. The human spirit rises above the mundane and is the source of all great cultural achievements of the human race. The spiritual includes the virtuous and ethical as well as a recognition of the dark or shadow side of human existence. The spiritual may, or may not, include the religious

---

[82]   Tarnas, op.cit., p. 70.

dimension, depending upon how one defines the term. The transcendent dimension deals with the ultimate questions of life. This spiritual dimension deals with the issues of meaning, purpose, and the overarching values of a culture.

The sixth category is the <u>psycho-social</u>, which is so comprehensive that one can scarcely do justice to it in a paragraph. Aristotle called man a social animal (<u>zoon politicon</u>).[83] The social needs of the human being are dictated by the fact that individuals are unable to exist for long in total isolation. From birth, some animals are instantly equipped to survive and develop on their own. Not so the human animal. There is an exceedingly long maturation curve for human offspring, extending from infancy to early adulthood. They require constant nurturing and care, especially, with reference to the educational and intellectual dimensions of life. The absence of social intercourse leaves a sense of loss and deprivation.

The seventh and final component is one which underlies all of the former categories, but cannot be subsumed under any one in particular. It is the <u>volitional nature</u> of the human being. Integral to an autonomous and productive life is the freedom to choose, the ability to shape one's own destiny. This involves the famous Four Freedoms of the former United States president Franklin Delano Roosevelt: freedom of speech, freedom to worship as one pleases, freedom of want, and freedom from fear.[84] These freedoms are implied in the

---

[83]   Aristotle, <u>Politics</u>, Bk. I, Chap. 2.

[84]   Four Freedoms: "We look forward to world founded upon four essential human freedoms. The first is freedom of speech and expression—everywhere in the world. The second is freedom of every person to worship God in his own way—everywhere in the world. The third is freedom of want . . . everywhere in the world. The fourth is freedom from fear . . . anywhere in the world." (Message to Congress by President Franklin Delano Roosevelt on January 6, 1941.)

basic triad of inalienable rights guaranteed by the United States Constitution: life, liberty and the pursuit of happiness.

> This brief survey of the wants and needs of the human soul gives some idea of the scope and size of the chasm, and why it takes so much to fill the inner void. And even when all of those wants and needs are met, humans are insatiable, they still want more. It is no wonder that the aspirations and needs of the human soul have been compared to the hungry maw of a black hole at the center of a galaxy, devouring everything that comes within its gravitational field.

As one can readily detect, any attempt to scale the size of the inner void soon reveals a vast chasm at the core of one's being that craves to be filled. The grandeur of man involves, not only the complex inner structures of selfhood—rationality, self-transcendence, self-awareness, freedom, the power to question, etc.—it also involves the highest and most noble aspirations of the human spirit. The inner void is an infinite abyss. No one can fully plumb its depths.

The problem addressed is one that is infinite—it has no bounds. Its dimensions seem impossible to scale since the problem is as big as life itself. Any treatment of the subject inevitably falls short of a complete analysis of the problem—let alone providing any final answer. Just when one has concluded that the job of discovery is finished, a new line of inquiry opens up, or an old line of inquiry proves incomplete.

It may be difficult to measure something so subjective; nevertheless, it is incumbent upon the inquirer to set some limits to the inquiry if one is to have anything meaningful to say at all. One must come to terms with this irresistably attractive issue, which is of such central importance to human existence. Consequently, this inquiry concerns itself only with those aspirations of the human spirit that have to do with a <u>holistic understanding</u> <u>of the self</u>. It treats only those urgent needs, which when satisfied, bring wholeness, completeness and happiness to one's existence.

The void in the human soul, which represents a deprivation and loss of meaning, results in angst and uneasiness. It drives the individual into frantic attempts to fill that void in their lives. Some employ finite and immediate means, such as: hedonism, wealth accumulation, the quest for fame and power, philanthropic endeavors, etc.

Others look to religion with its promise of infinite rewards; or, they seek a comprehensive secular philosophy, like humanism, for their ultimate answers. Each of these solutions to the human predicament will be examined in turn in the next section on **Filling the Inner Void**. They will be tested for their adequacy to fill that universal void within.

Chapter XI

FINITE ANSWERS

Humans have devised many different strategies to fill the inner void with something that they hope will answer to the feeling of emptiness in the human heart. One strategy is the pursuit of pleasure.

1. Pleasure

All men seek happiness; and, they seek to fill their lives with that which brings happiness. True, lasting happiness fills the void and solves the human problem; however, some persons confuse happiness with pleasure. Happiness is a long-term value; whereas, pleasure satisfies for the moment, but does not last. It is characterized by immediacy, fleeting satisfaction, and temporary gratification.

Countless commercial advertisements in the media recommend the use of a product for its immediate gratification. One is urged to: "Go for the gusto!" "Enjoy!" "Live it up because you only go around once!" "If you've got it, flaunt it!" "Go for it!" And, of course, there is the time-worn adage, "Eat, drink, and be merry, for tomorrow we die," which is at least as old as the seventh century BCE.[85]

---

[85] Isaiah 22:13.

Then there is the joke about the doctor who advised his patient that he has been having too much "wine, women and song" and that for his health's sake, he must give up something. The patient replied, "Ok, doc, I'll give up singing." People are reluctant to give up their pleasures, and that is all right because there is nothing wrong with pleasure. The problem arises when pleasure is made the primary goal of the individual. That is called "hedonism." It is living entirely for oneself and one's own pleasure-gratification.

The classic example of hedonism is the protagonist Don Juan in Tirso de Molina's play, <u>The Mocker of Seville and the Stone Guest</u> (1610). The Spanish dramatist established Don Juan as a sensual blasphemer and provided the plot for Mozart's <u>Don Giovanni</u>.

Don Juan was a dashing, dissolute, and irresistible rogue—a womanizer driven by boundless lust to conquer one woman after another. It was rumored that his conquests numbered in the thousands. He was dedicated to sensual pleasure and after each seduction, he abandons the woman and promptly goes on to another adventure, repeating that pattern all over 17th century Europe.

Probably, the most famous modern exponent of hedonism and the Don Juan lifestyle is Hugh Hefner of the <u>Playboy</u> magazine empire. Mr. Hefner has been a lifelong proponent of the sexually liberated lifestyle. He borrowed $600 and with nude photographs of Marilyn Monroe, the sex goddess of the sixties, he parlayed that into a multi-billion dollar empire promoting freedom of sexual expression.

Hefner opposed the oppressive anti-sexualism of the Victorian Age morality; instead, he celebrated the natural beauty of the human female body. His magazine always had a certain class about it as opposed to the trashy porno magazines that denigrated sex and the human body in favor of puerile interests, like Larry Flint's <u>Hustler</u> magazine.

Hefner's <u>Playboy</u> magazine always featured centerfolds and picture layouts of "the girl next door" (Everyone should have such neighbors). The magazine sought a more wholesome image of the female body and human sexuality in general. But the magazine was not just another "girlie" publication. It promoted an entire philosophy of life. It deliberately projected a cool, sophisticated image for the modern liberated male to emulate. Slick advertisements were geared to exploit this upbeat, free-wheeling, self-indulgent, male image. Nothing but the finest sports cars, high-tech toys, and the best bourbons and wines were tauted in the magazine.

In general, the image recommended for the modern male was that of a person somewhat aloof from long-term commitments with one's sexual partner. He was counseled to enjoy sex in an exploitative manner for one's self-gratification. The principal rule to be followed was to enjoy the sensual life to its fullest, only don't become involved in emotional entanglements. The Playboy philosophy is best illustrated by the cartoon that showed a young crew-cut male having wild foreplay with a luscious young chick and saying, "Why talk about love at a time like this?" Marriage and long-term commitments interfere with the full enjoyment and use of one's partner as a sex toy, according to the Playboy philosophy.

Hedonism sets one on a path that leads inevitably to despair. It follows a natural dialectic where too much of anything—even the greatest of pleasures—leads to boredom. For example, if one were to eat one's favorite food everyday for every meal, one would tire of it and no longer derive pleasure from it. Therefore, one seeks variety. "Variety is the spice of life," it is said. The gourmand knows how to vary his diet for maximum enjoyment. But eventually, no matter how great the pleasure might be, boredom sets in; and then, one must escalate one's desires to the next level, and the next, and the next, until one runs out of options or ends up in exhaustion. When there are no more options left, one faces the inevitable despair. For the human being, no finite pleasure can ultimately satisfy the complex needs of the human spirit.

The Hindu religion recognizes this and has a healthy strategy for dealing with pleasure. For the Hindu, pleasure is viewed as one of the good things in life. If one wants pleasure, the Hindu says, "Have at it!" They endorse enjoying life's pleasures to the max; but then, they sit back and wait. Ultimately, the individual will tire of that course in life. Pleasure is not enough to satisfy the higher needs of the human soul. When we come to that crucial juncture in life, we are ready for the next level, which in the Hindu religion is a life dedicated to success, which involves contributing responsibly to the community. In short, it is living according to duty and fulfilling our obligations to others.

This approach is reminiscent of the philosophy of the Danish Christian existentialist Soren Kierkegaard in his <u>Stages on Life's Way</u>. Kierkegaard begins with the initial stage, which is characterized by hedonism. He calls this the aesthetic stage because the pleasures sought might be those found in the arts and literature, as well as in a life of sensuality. The dialectic of the aesthetic stage is, nevertheless, the same in both kinds of pleasure-seeking: hedonism leads to boredom, which is followed by an escalation of pleasures; then more boredom; and ultimately, it leads to exhaustion of the options, which then, leads to despair.

Despair drives us on to the next stage, which for Kierkegaard, is the ethical stage. That is where the Don Juan settles down and gets married. He takes up a responsible role in society and fulfills his duty to home, community and the nation. There is an inevitable progression from the aesthetic stage to the ethical because hedonism in the long run fails to satisfy the complex needs of the human spirit.

For Hugh Hefner, our modern day Don Juan, the lifestyle of uncommitted sexual freedom eventually proved unsatisfying—even for the King of Sensuality. What Hefner, as a man, really wanted was the warmth and security of a loving home and family. He eventually married one of his centerfold playmates and gave up his free-wheeling lifestyle to raise a family and be a loyal husband. That was what Hef really wanted and ultimately found—at least for awhile. Sadly, the marriage ended in divorce with his wife getting custody of the two boys; but, that was not what the King really wanted.

Hedonism is not the most rewarding lifestyle. At best, it is a preliminary stage to what the human being really wants—the love and security for a home and family.

2. Wealth

"Money alone sets the world in motion" according to Publius Syrus (1ˢᵗ century BCE).[86] That adage is descriptive of the fact that with the introduction of money as a medium of exchange, everything had a monetary value placed on it. Everything could be bought for a price. Aristotle described how money replaced the old style barter and swap market where values were often difficult to establish.

With the advent of money, the trading posts used as its new currency (the coins of the realm) as a means for buying and selling. With the introduction of money, wealth could be stored for future use. Wealth-accumulation permitted capital formation to trade on a stock exchange for shares in commodities or interests in companies that were publicly listed for trading purposes. The free market would determine the value placed on the shares listed on the stock exchange.

The hedonist soon learned that pleasure-seeking costs money. If persons are going to fulfill their desires, then they need a source of income. The expensive toys sought by the hedonist like sports cars, yachts, a stylish wardrobe, gourmet

---

[86]   Maxiim 656, Publius Syrus, 1ˢᵗ century BCE, quoted in Pliny <u>Natural History</u>, 35, sec. 199.

dining, the latest high-tech gadgets, etc., all cost money. Unless one has a rich uncle, in order to obtain money—outside of criminal activity—one must find employment or go into business. When one takes this step, then one enters the interconnectedness of the social and financial communities. This requires the adoption of a new strategy. No longer can one act simply for one's own personal satisfaction and the immediacy of instant gratification. Success in business involves the acceptance of the fact that if one expects to be rewarded financially, one must offer a service that is valued by the community. If one is to build a reputation for offering goods and services with efficiency and integrity, the individual must think in a wider context than one's immediate self-interest. True, one may be in business for reasons of self-interest, but that cannot be the whole story. One must always keep the customer's interest foremost in mind, i.e., if one's business is to thrive and succeed. Business transactions are a <u>quid pro quo</u>. One must give equal value, if one is to receive compensation in return. The change in attitude from pure hedonism to the world of business is profound. The individual becomes a responsible citizen of the community and lives by the ethical code and moral values of that society. In other words, one accepts the duties and obligations which promote the welfare of others.

In the Hindu society, the move from hedonism to the life of duty and moral obligation is definitely considered to be a higher, more satisfying life than that of the isolated individual. Thus wealth accumulation requires social involvement, human values, and a commitment to others.

The problem of greed and exploitation of the system always is a danger; but, by-and-large, society has its means of dealing with unethical conduct.

The Bible says that "the love of money is the root of all evil";[87] but that is not a condemnation of money or the monetary system, as such. It is critical of the inordinate lust

---

[87]   II Timothy 6:10.

for money that causes one to violate the rights and interests of others. Greed knows no bounds, because the human being thinks more of self-interest and self-aggrandizement than of the best interests of his or her peers. Enlightened capitalism depends on an underlying business ethic and established moral values in the community. Money <u>per se</u> is not the root of evil; it is the <u>love</u> of money, the <u>lust</u> for money, that is the cause of evil. Money may not bring happiness; but then, neither does poverty. Money is neither good nor evil. It is a neutral means of exchange.

No matter how much money one has, it is never enough; one always wants more. Perhaps, some multi-billionaires have so far surpassed the point of satisfying their personal comfort level that they give some of their excess funds to worthy causes; but that sort of philanthropy will be examined in due course. However, these philanthropists do not halt their money-making machines and say that they don't want to earn any more money. No, they still fight for dominance in their given industry and seek to maintain their revenue stream. There is never enough money to do all that one desires.

In the final analysis, "You can't take it with you," as the saying goes. Money is fleeting and cannot bring lasting happiness. One recalls the image of the multi-billionaire William Randolph Hearst sitting in his huge mansion amidst opulence and splendor at San Simeon and mourning over the loss of his lifetime companion, Marion Davies, by playing over and over again old film clips of his deceased lover. No amount of money can restore the loss of a loved one, and no amount of money can fill the void left in the human heart by that loss.

3. Fame

Fame and fortune naturally seem to go together; however, this need not be the case. Witness someone like Mahatmas Gandhi, who owned nothing but the homespun loincloth that he wore; yet, his fame is renowned worldwide. Nevertheless, given what humans are, they naturally gravitate toward those who are both rich <u>and</u> famous; that is, for those who have made it big in the eyes of the world. Fame and fortune are sought as major values by the popular masses. The rich and famous always seem to have lots of friends. Everyone wants to be around them. The adage, "It's not what you know, it's who you know," sums up the common notion that some of the power and influence of the famous might rub off on a person by just being around them. For the name dropper, it seems to be a badge of honor to be able to say, "I know such-and-such famous person." On the other hand, the song, "Nobody knows you when you're down and out," sums up the opposite situation.

In Tinseltown, the world of make-believe, even to be nominated for an Oscar award is automatically to share in the fame and notoriety of the winner. And, to be the Honoree at the Kennedy Center for Performing Arts is the epitome of an actor's or musician's career. It means respect and adulation from one's peers and from the public. At one time, there was a long-running television program called, "The Rich and Famous." For one to be featured on that program was to be doubly famous; because then, one was famous for being famous.

Humans are constantly looking for role models that they can admire and emulate. They become "groupies" of the famous, whether they be rock stars or movie stars. "Stardom" is an appellation that indicates one shines brighter than everyone else around them. These "stars" become the public's "guiding lights," and often their moral compass. They can do no wrong in the eyes of the public.

People have a deep-seated desire to be known, to be a "somebody." They dread being a "nobody," and will do practically anything for their fifteen minutes of fame. This is especially true of those with low self-esteem. They want to feel important.

In Arthur Miller's play, "The Death of a Salesman," the principal character, Willy Loman, was a hack salesman with dreams of grandeur. He favored his elder son, Biff, because he had been a star high school athlete. Even though Biff was now an unemployed drifter, Willy thought of him as the "greatest" because once he had been a gridiron star. Willy told Biff that the really important thing in life was to be liked—<u>well</u> liked. Willy Loman symbolizes all those with misplaced values who worship at the altar of the "Bitch Goddess of Fame and Success."

Fame is a heady thing. It, like power, is an aphrodisiac. Public adulation can make persons feel more powerful and important than they really are. For some, it "goes to their head," so that they become over-bearing and arrogant, despising the "little people" around them. But fame is a fleeting thing. The public is fickle and can turn on a person in a heartbeat. In the film industry, there is a saying, "Be good to those you meet on the way up, because you will meet them again on the way down."

At the coronation of each new pope, the papal celebrants, when in procession, chant, <u>Sic transit gloria mundi</u> (so passes away the glory of this world). The Pope is reminded by this warning that all of the adulation and splendor and trappings of the papal office are a fleeting and temporary thing. It will soon pass away.

Fame is an elusive and finite value. It, like pleasure and wealth, has its moments of glory; but, one's self-esteem should never be built upon it, because when it departs, then one has nothing left. All that remains of that person is a hollow shell. Fame has its rewards, but it is insufficient to fill one's life with lasting satisfaction. It, like wealth and power, can be lost over night. Like all finite values, fame will not sustain the human soul with the meaning that it requires.

4. Power

According to Friedrich Nietzsche, power is the name of the game. In his book, <u>The Will to Power</u>, Nietzsche put forth the thesis that power is what life is all about. There are those with the natural ability to command a following and lead the masses; and, there are those born to follow. The goal in life is to accumulate as much power and prestige as possible. That is a sign of strength of character. If it be necessary to trample upon the weak, so be it. Nietzsche wrote that it was inevitable that some superior persons, whom he called "Supermen," would dominate others. They were endowed with the natural talents to exercise power, and it was their destiny to do so.

In the financial arena, Nietzsche would probably have endorsed <u>laisse faire</u> capitalism, where the struggle to dominate the economic competition could be played out to its fullest extent without restraint. That monetary system is the epitome of the struggle for power. Amassing large amounts of capital is paramount, for therein lies <u>real power</u> to control and dominate others.

In the political arena, it is raw power that succeeds, because only those with the fortitude to crush their potential rivals and impose their will upon others, will survive. There is no room for fair play or moderation in the exercise of power.

According to Nietzsche, the Christian ethic is a "slave ethic." It counsels the individual to subordinate his/her best interests to that of the other. Jesus of Nazareth taught, "Whoever slaps you on your right cheek, turn the other cheek to him also." "Whoever compels you to go one mile, go with him two." "If someone steals your tunic, let him have your cloak also." "Love your enemies, and bless those that curse you, do good to those who hate you, and pray for those who spitefully use you."[88] Nietzsche heaped scorn on that submissive slave mentality. Pacifism in face of power is an invitation to suicide. The pacifism of someone like Gandhi, or Martin Luther King, Jr., works only in a context where a government respects a certain code of behavior based upon conscience. Ruthless power like that wielded by the Hitlers

---

[88] Matthew 5:23-42.

and Stalins of the world has no patience with that sort of weakness.

But, power can be lost. It is fleeting and transitory. As has been mentioned, at every coronation of a pope, the procession charges, "So passes away the glory of this world." The pope is counseled: Life is short; power is fleeting; therefore, use it wisely.

Nietzsche recognized the temporary nature of power, but he took comfort in the myth of eternal recurrence; where history repeats itself over and over again in the vast sweep of time, so that power lost eventually will be restored. It never seemed to bother Nietzsche that this event may not reoccur again for an infinite amount of time in human reckoning.

As Nietzsche wrote, some people are natural leaders and destined to rule. Simply by the force of their personalities they command a following. Usually, these persons exhibit superiority in mental, physical and social skills so that their natural talents are obvious to all. Their political instincts are flawless so that they have a natural ability to garner power and influence. They usually are persons of immense talent and charisma, often with a keen mind and oratorical ability. But above all, they are persons with great ambition and drive who have the moxie, the "know-how" to get their way.

Of such a person was Gaius Julius Caesar, who became Emperor of the Roman Empire in 46 BCE. It was obvious from the "get-go" that this gifted and ruthlessly ambitious young man was destined to rule. The then Dictator, Sulla, warned the eminent members of the aristocratic party that Caesar would "one day prove the ruin of the party which you and I have so long defended."[89] Soothsayers also pronounced that one day Caesar would rule the world.

Julius Caesar was in many ways a superior general and a courageous leader in battle. He often led his troops personally into battle under extremely adverse conditions. He was

---

[89]   Suetonius, The Twelve Caesars, p. 10.

physically powerful, with great stamina and endurance. He led his troops by sheer exercise of his personal authority. He was a superb tactician and knew how to take advantage of the enemy's weaknesses. When routing his opponents, he gave no quarter for them to regroup. Consequently, he seldom lost a battle.

In the political arena, Caesar had a natural talent for intrigue; he manipulated the system to his advantage and enjoyed playing the game of power broker. He knew how to buy influence and to win the popular opinion. He was a shrewd politician and a master at controlling the situation. He seldom let ethics or religion deter him for a moment. He was amoral in his personal life, but a strict disciplinarian with others.

Julius Caesar was an ambitious power-grabber, an unprincipled manipulator of the levers of power. His machinations behind the scenes won him the necessary alliances to succeed. The constant exercise of power gave Caesar the love of it. Unfortunately, Caesar succumbed to the disease—the lust for power. It was not enough to be head of State; he demanded to be treated as a god. Indeed, he declared himself to be divine and even founded a new college of Lupercals to celebrate his divinity.

When, as a general, he became disenchanted with the Roman Senate and his inability to control that body, he decided on a course of civil war. He led his troops across a bridge over the Rubicon, a river separating Gaul and Italy, and said, "The die is cast." He marched on Rome, overthrowing the government and naming himself Emperor and absolute Dictator of the Roman Empire. The swiftness of the victory was proclaimed by a banner on a parade wagon: veni, vidi, vici (I came, I saw, I conquered). Caesar proclaimed that the Republic was nothing—a mere name without form or substance. He scorned the Constitution and proclaimed his word as law.

Caesar, according to Suetonius, demanded and accepted: the title of Emperor, a lifetime dictatorship, a life-consulship, the title of "Father of his country" the renaming of the seventh month of the year as "July" to memorialize his name forever, divine status, and a golden throne in the Senate from which he ruled with absolute power.

Power is an aphrodisiac; one can become drunk with power. To have unlimited power is to be like a god, and that was exactly what Caesar sought. Power goes to one's head; and when there is no restrainer, it becomes tyrannical. Absolute power cannot long be tolerated by the people. The rest of the story, about how several Senators banded together to assassinate Caesar and restore the Republic, is history.

Julius Caesar was a prime example of Lord Acton's warning: "Power tends to corrupt. Absolute power corrupts absolutely."[90] Absolute power becomes intolerable. Power, like all other finite values, must eventually be relinquished. There never was enough power to fill the void in the human heart; therefore, the situation ends in despair or death.

5. Knowledge

"Knowledge is power," wrote Sir Francis Bacon in the 17th century, and never was it more true than today in this, the 21st century.[91] We live in a high-tech age where highly sophisticated knowledge is essential. The movement from an agrarian economy in the 16th and 17th centuries; to an industrial one in the 18th and 19th centuries; then, to a technological society in the 20th and 21st centuries was the result of an explosion of knowledge so that we are now known as homo technologicus. Knowledge has proven useful

---

90   Lord John Emerich Acton, Letter to Bishop Mendell Creighton [April 5, 1887].

91   Bacon, Francis, Meditationes Sacrae, [1597] De Haeresibus.

in bettering the human condition; and that was how Bacon presented his case for acquiring knowledge. It was measured in terms of what it could do for mankind. Knowledge was valued because it improved the lot of human beings. Today, that is still the bottom line in most pleas for research grants.

When it comes to the issue of knowledge that has no immediate practical application, one often hears the question raised: Why spend time and money on useless knowledge? An example of such a question would be: Why spend billions of dollars on space hardware like the Hubble and James Webb Space Telescope?[92] Of what value is it to know about distant stars and galaxies? Wouldn't it be better to spend that money on improving the school system?

This raises the critical question as to the value of fundamental research and the value of knowledge <u>per se</u>. Does knowledge have value only in pragmatic applications, or is it intrinsically worthwhile?

Aristotle wrote in his <u>Metaphysics</u>, "All men by nature want to know."[93] In other words, the human animal has an insatiable need to know. It wants to know the truth regardless of its practical consequences and pragmatic value.

Knowledge liberates the human mind from the bondage of superstition and oppressive institutions. A classic example of that is found in the person of Galileo. He turned a six inch telescope constructed by himself on the night sky; and thereby revolutionized the way that humans understand both themselves and their world. There was no immediate practical benefit from his discovery; but he emancipated humankind from an overbearing, authoritarian institution that tried to control what could or could not be taught. He liberated humankind from the bondage of superstition and ignorance.

---

[92]   The Hubble Space Telescope is to be followed by the James Webb Space Telescope which will be designed to search the Ultra Deep field of outer space.

[93]   Aristotle, <u>Metaphysics</u>, Bk. I, Ch. 1.

Now, when it comes to the issue of whether to spend vast sums on space exploration and optical instruments like the Hubble telescope, the reply to the critics can only be the same as in Galileo's day: It has given us the <u>universe</u>! Galileo widened the human mind and perspective by revealing the frightful immensity of the universe. We have learned something that we otherwise would not have known— something that has revolutionized the way that humans understand themselves.

When the question is raised about whether the money might have been better spent on schools, the reply must be: what would one teach in those schools without the knowledge gained from basic research into the nature of the Cosmos? Would one be content with a pre-Copernican, pre-Galilean world view; or, a pre-Hubble universe?

The liberating function of knowledge cannot be measured in pragmatic or quantitative terms. It sets the mind free to soar, to imagine and to create. The exercise of free inquiry has been the magic command of "Open Sesame" for the human race. It has released untold treasures of new knowledge. It has brought creativity and innovation onto the human stage.

For the individual, there is never enough knowledge. There is always one more thing needed to complete one's understanding. One always seeks new intellectual fields to conquer; but there is never enough time or energy to learn what one needs to know. Knowledge is perhaps the most satisfying of all the finite answers that humankind uses to fill the void within the self. It is something of lasting value. Once one has learned something new, no one can take it away. It becomes a part of who one is. Yet, in and of itself, knowledge alone is not enough to satisfy the human heart. Apart from a social context to share one's insights, knowledge can become empty and unrewarding. It fails to satisfy the complex needs of the human soul.

Faust is a case in point. Goethe, in his play <u>Faust</u>, tells of a university professor with all of the necessary academic credentials and years of teaching experience to be recognized as an authority in his field. But Faust became disenchanted with the learning of his day. It left too many questions unanswered. His old, dry, dusty books seemed only to rehash the same old arguments. He grew restless and desired to break beyond the bonds of human finitude. With the assistance of the demonic Mephistopheles, he sought universal knowledge and wisdom; but at the price of selling his soul to the Devil.

Ultimately, Faust realized that all of the knowledge, power, and pleasure of the world were not enough to make him truly happy. In Goethe's version of <u>Faust</u>, his soul was rescued by turning his great intellectual acumen to projects that benefit humankind. Faust discovered that intellect and brain power alone are not enough to satisfy the human heart. It is only rewarding when made to serve the best interests of human society.

6. Philanthropy

The natural dialectic of life, according to Kierkegaard, drives one from the aesthetic stage to the ethical stage. Philanthropy is one form of behavior that represents the ethical stage. Through financial generosity, the donor endeavors to alleviate the pain and suffering of the less fortunate. Philanthropists are also known for funding large social projects in the community interest.

The Rockefeller family, for example, is a financial dynasty that has been extremely successful in the business of oil production. John D. Rockefeller, Sr. founded the Standard Oil Company, which has been a huge revenue-producing company, making the Rockefellers immensely wealthy. The Rockefellers are an exception to the norm in that they have felt a responsibility to give back to the community a portion of what they received. As a result, they have funded countless philanthropic causes, which have benefited the entire world.

There is an element of self-interest to their philanthropy in that they channel monies through charitable foundations in order to receive huge tax-relief benefits. Thus their giving is a rational decision made out of enlightened self-interest. That, however, does not detract from their inordinate generosity and sense of social responsibility.

In our time, there are the Bill Gates, the Warren Buffets and the Ted Turners of the world who have so far surpassed any need of further creature comforts for themselves that they have been willing to give back to the community financial support for many noble causes—not only for their own country, but for the needy throughout the world. Ted Turner gave the United Nations a sum of 38 million dollars when it was in a budget crisis; and Bill Gates gave 35 million to India for AIDS prevention. Gates' entire fortune of some forty billion dollars has been placed in the Bill and Melinda Gates Foundation, "Dedicated to the idea that all people deserve the chance to live a healthy, productive life." Its goal is to eradicate disease worldwide. And Warren Buffet has pledged his fortune of some fifty billion dollars to the Gates Foundation. These people are extraordinary. They have a strong commitment to the society that permitted them to become billionaires.

Philanthropists, as has been noted, do not part with their hard, cold cash entirely out of altruism. For instance, most large donors to a college or university want their names on a building, or to have it connected with an endowment for a departmental chair, providing the salary for a professorship. Self-aggrandizement is a major factor for rich donors. They desire to immortalize their names by giving lavish gifts to charitable causes. Not only does this raise their community esteem, it guarantees their remembrance in perpetuity.

The problem for the individual in the ethical stage is that the need is infinite, but resources are finite. As Jesus of

Nazareth once said, "The poor are with us always." No matter how many persons one helps, there are always millions more starving and deprived of the basic human necessities. The problem is systemic, especially in a world without population control. The need always outstrips the ability to produce enough to go around equitably.

A prime example of this sad situation was Oskar Schindler, of the book and movie, <u>Schindler's List</u>. Schindler was a German industrial entrepreneur during the Second World War. He was interested in amassing a great fortune by taking advantage of the Nazi exploitation of the Jewish population. Schindler was an extraordinarily shrewd confidence man and manipulator of people. He persuaded wealthy Jews to lend him huge sums of money (that would have been confiscated by the Nazis anyway) in order to build an enamelware factory designed to employ Jewish persons eligible for deportation to the concentration camps. This endeavor was designed to save Jewish lives; and, hopefully, to bring profits to the investors.

Over the course of time, as the war progressed and Jews were being shipped wholesale to their inevitable death in the crematoria of Auschwitz, Dachau, Bergen-Belsen, Buchenwald, etc., Schindler used his great influence with the Nazi party officials and military personnel through bribes, payoffs and favor to protect his factory workers from being carted away to concentration camps.

Eventually, he became so committed to the Jewish cause that he would pay huge sums of money out of his personal profits to spare the life of every Jew he could possibly save. After he had spent all of his fortune on this mission of mercy, he sat down and cried because he could do no more. When he looked at the gold wedding ring on his finger, he felt great pangs of guilt because, as he said, "If I'd only sold my ring, I could've saved one more life."

Oskar Schindler represents the dilemma of the individual who, although motivated by the duty of the ethical stage, can never do enough to alleviate the pain and suffering in the world.[94] One's sense of duty to humanity inevitably leads to frustration, guilt, exhaustion, and eventually, despair. That dialectic, according to Kiekegaard, is what drives one on from the ethical to the religious stage, which will be considered in the next section.

---

[94]   For a less flattering view of Oskar Schindler, see David Crowe, <u>Oskar Schindler, The Untold Account of His Life</u>, (Elon University, North Carolina, 2004).

Chapter XII

RELIGIOUS ANSWERS

Humans universally experience a sense of emptiness, a craving within the human soul. They attempt to fill that inner void with various forms of escapism: hedonism, fame and fortune, mindless activity, compulsive economic consumption, spectator sports, cults, fadism, alcoholism, drug addiction and trivia-filled lives. However, none of these finite values are able to satisfy the infinite void within. They all leave a gnawing spiritual hunger. It is like the person described by the prophet Isaiah who dreamed that he was enjoying a great feast— eating and drinking to his heart's content, "But when he awakens . . . his soul is still hungry."[95] Those who turn to that which is transient and finite to satisfy the inner longing find out that the soul still craves for something more. The soul is left with a spiritual void—empty, unsatisfied and unfulfilled.

We have noted how the Hebrew sage and author of Ecclesiastes conducted an experiment in the laboratory of life to find out what could bring lasting satisfaction. He concluded that nothing finite could satisfy the infinite longing in the human soul, i.e., nothing "under the sun". The sage gave a reason for his negative appraisal of the human situation. He wrote, "God (Elohim) has put eternity

---

[95] Isaiah 29:8.

(<u>olam</u>) in their hearts."[96] That is a poetic way of saying that humans have been endowed with the capacity to conceive the infinite, the eternal; hence, nothing finite can satisfy. Having "eternity" in their minds meant that they could grasp concepts like the infinite, absolute, unlimited, all-encompassing, ultimate reality, etc. No longer could their questions be confined to merely finite, pragmatic concerns.

Mankind's powers of inquiry extend beyond the finite to the asking of questions about things ultimate. People want to know: Where did I come from? Why am I here? What is the meaning of my life? How should I live? Is there a moral order? How does one explain the existence of evil? What is its source? What can I hope? Is there immortality of the soul, i.e., personal existence beyond the grave? How should one act in face of the mysterious unknown—the void which surrounds and penetrates the human soul? These persistent questions plague the human mind and cause anguish. They become the source of the religious quest.

Religion is the attempt to answer mankind's ultimate questions. It is based upon the notion that only something infinite can fill the infinite void within the human soul. That infinite reality has been variously described as: Elohim, the Spirit of Yahweh (Lord), Theos (God), Krishna, Christ, the Great Spirit, the Buddha Spirit, Allah, Tao, etc. Religion is the human attempt to put a face on that infinite nameless void. Through religion, humans seek to comprehend the world in its mystery and magnitude. They seek to domesticate that which is essentially irrational, chaotic, unknowable and threatening to their very being.

---

[96]   Eccl. 3:11. The <u>imago</u> <u>dei </u>of Genesis 1:26, 27 would imply a "sense of the eternal."

The religious quest is as old as the human race. According to Rudolf Bultmann, the German scholar of primitive religions,

> Mankind, from his earliest days, was anxious before the unknown. He sought to placate the mysterious and hostile forces of nature by means of ritual and magic.[97]

The quest to comprehend the mysterious unknown is found in the prehistoric burial rites of homo sapiens. Archaeological discoveries have unearthed fossil bones of early humans who lived over 100,000 years ago. They buried their dead with food, weapons and personal items to be used by the departed in an afterlife. They covered their dead with flowers and painted their faces with red ochre to simulate health and vitality. It was obvious that internment of the deceased was a sacred rite which was considered preparation for a journey into another world.

That concern for the mysterious unknown is found in the magic and rituals used by aboriginal tribes in their attempt to control mana, the powers and forces of nature. Rudolf Otto, in his epochal work, The Idea of the Holy, points out how religion very early was the attempt of humans to deal with the mysterium tremendum, the tremendous mystery that lies behind all that is. Humans stand in awe before the overwhelming forces of a world that seems opaque and virtually impossible to penetrate or comprehend.

1. Religion in Ancient Greece

The longing for an infinite answer is found throughout human history. Plato, in the Timaeus, recounts the Orphic myth about the origin of the human condition. He wrote that

---

[97]   Rudolph Bultmann, Jesus Christ and Mythology, p.

in the beginning, human souls were created by the gods as perfect beings, each inhabiting its own star in the celestial dome. The souls, however, fell from Heaven to earth passing through the orbits of the planetary gods, thus acquiring their vices. By the time that the souls had arrived on earth, they had already been corrupted by the evils acquired on their long journey: so that human history was constantly filled with turmoil and wars. Yet each soul subconsciously realized that this was not its natural state. It had a longing, or "homesickness" for Heaven and its original state of perfection. Only by living two exemplary lives, said Plato, could the soul return to its home in the stars. There it would live once more in a state of bliss. This Orphic myth recounted by Plato was the Greek way of speaking about the void within the human soul.

"Homesickness" was the experience of being estranged, cut off, alienated from one's true home and destiny. The feeling was an awareness that life was out of joint and that one's true destiny was with the gods in the heavens. This, essentially, was a religious answer to the human condition. The salvation of the human soul lay not on this earth, but in the celestial realm with the gods. That was the soul's true destiny. The Orphic myth held all of the elements of a religious answer to the human predicament: the creation of humans in a state of innocence and perfection; a Fall into sin and corruption; an explanation for the origin of evil; estrangement and alienation; a longing for one's true homeland in the Heavens; a plan of salvation; and finally, the eventual reunion with the gods in Heaven.

This homesickness for Heaven gets reflected in Plato's doctrine of Recollection. Knowledge is simply recollection in that the mind remembers the realm of transcendent Ideas where truth, goodness and beauty were experienced in their fullness from the discarnate existence before birth when the soul lived among the gods. For example, the soul knows intuitively what justice, virtue and wisdom are because it still can dimly recall these universal Forms stored in its memory.

Education, for Plato, was not stuffing the mind with facts; rather, it was a process of recovering what was already stored there. The recollection of those memories from a prior existence in Heaven was the goal of education. The term <u>education</u> comes from two Latin words <u>e</u> and <u>ducere</u>, meaning, "to lead out." Socrates' teaching style was to disavow that he had anything to impart to his hearers, asserting that he could only elicit from his hearers what was already latent in their minds through the process of dialectical reasoning and questioning, i.e., discursive reasoning. Socrates acted as a midwife for human souls, helping them deliver the truth that lay within the soul's interior depths. In seeing beauty, according to Plato, the soul is stirred to recollection of that purer beauty, that more real beauty it had known in Heaven. Thus knowledge of Beauty and the other Eternal Forms is simply a recollection of Heaven.

Alcibiades, in Plato's <u>Symposium</u>, compared Socrates to a figurine of Silenus which was sold in the statuary shops of Athens. They were made to open in the middle, which then revealed an image of god inside it. These divine golden images within the Silenus statue represented to the ancient Greeks the reality that every person could be a god-bearer. This concept that one could be "in-dwelt" by a god was also reflected in their word of "enthusiasm," which comes from two Greek words, <u>en</u>-<u>theos</u>, meaning "god within." A person who was a god-bearer exhibited the exuberant, joyful enthusiasm of one who was "god-possessed." The Greek poet Ibycus was described as "full of god."[98] Edwin Irwin writes,

---

[98]   Bulfinch, <u>Mythology</u> (New York: Dill Publishing Co., 1951), p. 161.

"Plato knew these moments of 'enthusiasm' in the old Greek sense of 'being filled with a god.'"[99]

If the in-dwelling god were Eros, then one became a lover. If the god were Dionysius (god of wine and vineyards), then one manifested god-intoxicated, aesthetic rapture, and joyful happiness associated with the drinking of wine. The Greeks had a proverb, <u>In vino veritas</u>, which meant, "in wine is truth."[100] After a glass of wine the tongue becomes loosened and it speaks freely about what is in the heart.

Often alcoholic drinks are called "spirits." This derives from the notion that to be filled with the divine spirit brings the same god-intoxicated freedom and spontaneity as experienced in drinking wine. In fact, the Latin word for "inspiration" means to be "in-spirited," that is to be in-dwelt by a god (to be a god-bearer).

Socrates often spoke of his <u>daimon</u> that inspired him and gave him boldness to speak the truth. Socrates' daimon and the eleven Muses were intermediary spirits that conveyed messages to and from the gods. The Muses inspired all sorts of artistic and cultural endeavors from poetry and music to astronomy and wisdom. To be seized by one's Muse, was to be inspired above and beyond what was normally possible. Every writer understands what it means to be seized by the Muse Erato. He or she may suffer from "writer's block" where it seems that one has nothing to say; but then, when one is touched by the Muse, ideas and words begin to flow effortlessly in a frenzy of creativity. Where previously, everything was dark and dense, suddenly, one has insight and clarity. Creative juices begin to flow and the words come tumbling out like a waterfall. The Muse brings inspiration, vision and purpose. Socrates called this a "divine madness." It was indispensable for the artist, and without it, no striving or

---

99   Irwin, op.cir., p. xxxi.
100   Plato, <u>The Symposium</u>, 217.

effort would bring about any great work of art or philosophy. Socrates emphatically stated that

> He who having no touch of the Muses' madness
> in his soul, comes to the door and thinks that he
> will get into the temple with the help of art—he,
> I say, and his poetry are not admitted.[101]

Being smitten by one's Muse was a religious experience for the Greeks. It meant becoming a god-bearer. The Muse gave the artist or writer a mystical experience of beauty which enabled him or her to be creative. Poetry, for the Greeks, was a matter of participation in the divine and sharing in the power of the gods. Socrates said of the poets, "god himself is the speaker and through him he is conversing with us."[102]

But the experience of being a god-bearer was not just for poets and artists; it was something for everyone in that it inspired a virtuous life. To be god-possessed was to be filled with the Good, which meant living an ethical life.

2. Christianity

The essence of the Christian answer to the void in the human soul is the indwelling presence of God. For the Christian religion, this takes on the form of "Christ-mysticism." The only cure for the human malady is to be in-dwelt by the "Living Christ." One finds this Christ-mysticism typically in the Pauline epistles: "Christ in you, the hope of glory"[103]; and also, in the Johannine corpus: "He who abides in me and I in him bears much fruit."[104] The classical

---

[101] Ibid., p. 185.

[102] Ibid., p. xxxi.

[103] Colossians 1:27.

[104] John 15:5.

statement is found in The Revelation to John, "Behold, I stand at the door and knock. If anyone hears my voice and opens the door, I will come into him and dine with him and he with me."[105] Thus the answer to the void within is the "indwelling Christ."

Christ-mysticism seems to have originated with the Apostle Paul's reinterpretation of the Hebrew concept of Yahweh dwelling in the midst of his people, viz., in his tabernacle. The Mosaic Torah reads:

> **"I will set my tabernacle among you . . .**
>
> I will walk among you and be your
> God and you shall be my people."[106]

In the Hebrew Torah, Yahweh dwells among his people in the corporate sense. The Spirit of Yahweh, in the Torah, is always referred to as dwelling with the people in the plural, as a corporate body. The above passage gets reinterpreted by Paul who writes:

> "For we are the temple of the living God.
> As God has said:
> 'I will dwell in them
> And walk with them.
> I will be their God,
> And they shall be my people.'"[107] (emphasis added)

What was understood by the Hebrews as the presence of Yahweh in the collective Hebrew community, Paul personalized and individualized. It was Paul's personalizing of that corporate concept that led to his saying:

---

[105]   Rev. 3:20.

[106]   Leviticus 16:12.

[107]   II Corinthians 6:16.

"Christ <u>lives in me</u>."[108]
"the Spirit <u>in you</u>."[109]
"that Christ may <u>dwell in your hearts</u>."[110]

Paul's Christ-mysticism was essentially the same answer that Augustine gave to the human problem. In his <u>Confessions</u>, he stated that the human soul is "restless until it rests in Thee, O God."[111] This "restlessness" for the divine is analogous to Plato's "homesickness of the soul." In each case, there is an awareness that life is incomplete, that there is something missing, and only a divine presence will suffice.

In the 17th century, Blaise Pascal, a scientist and Christian mystic, wrote in his <u>Penses</u> (<u>Meditations</u>) that "man has a God-shaped vacuum in his heart and only God can fill that vacuum."[112] The "God-shaped vacuum" was Pascal's way of expressing the void-within. It was an infinite void that could be filled only with an infinite Spirit, namely God. This again, was the "homesickness" of Plato where there is a longing for an answer and only an infinite solution will do. Finite answers only disappoint and leave one empty and unsatisfied.

3. Hindu-Mysticism

The Hindu religion is based upon a similar concept of the inner presence of the divine, except that one is already indwelt by the divine. One's inmost being is called Atman. Atman is one's essential self, which is identified with Brahman, the ultimate principle and reality of the universe. The individual is not only indwelt by the divine; it is divine. The Hindu's

---

[108] Galatians 2:20.
[109] Galatians 3:5.
[110] Ephesians 3:17.
[111] St. Augustine, <u>Confessions</u>, I:8.
[112] Pascal, <u>Pensees</u>. Op. Cit., p.

have a saying, <u>Tat-tvam-asi</u> (That art thou), where the "That" is Brahman, and the "thou" is one's Atman. One's Atman is not separate from the ultimate Brahman. It is like a droplet of water that finds its way to the sea. Once part of the vast ocean, it is no longer distinguishable from the totality. So it is with the individual Atman. The self is part of the Self, or World Soul. In order to realize who one is, one needs to take an inner journey to discover one's true Atman nature.

As soon as one attempts to make any statement about the Hindu religion, one soon learns that there is something in their scriptures that seems to express the opposite. The reason is that Hinduism is an eclectic religion that includes many different pathways to the one ultimate goal—that of union with Ultimate Reality, with Brahman.

One path is that of <u>bhakti-marga</u>, the path of personal devotion to <u>Krishna</u>. This teaching is found in the <u>Upanishads</u>, and more particularly, in the <u>Mahabharata</u> and the <u>Bhagavad Gita</u>. Here the goal is to discover the presence of Krishna in one's heart: "Seeking me <u>in your heart</u>, you will at last be united with me."[113] (emphasis added).

In the Upanishad, it is written that sages can literally see the Love of God within themselves. It was he who lived in the heart of every creature and who ruled over space, time and causality. Know him, believers were advised, to be enshrined in your heart. Meditate and realize the world is filled with the Word of God. In their teaching, there was nothing more to know about life.

For Hindus who follow that path of devotion (<u>bhakti-marga</u>), the experience of <u>moksha</u> (ultimate union) involves a complete surrender to Krishna. For persons who find it difficult to conceive of an impersonal World Soul, i.e., Brahman, it gets personalized in the devotion to Krishna. Krishna is the avatar (incarnation) of Vishnu who, along with Brahma and Shiva, comprise the Hindu Triad of gods. They

---

[113]   <u>Bhagavad Gita</u>, 9.34.

are the highest expression of Ultimate Reality—of Brahman, the impersonal Soul of the World.

The accessibility of Krishna, the personification of God, accounts for the wide acceptance of the bhakti path to salvation. Therefore, in Hinduism, like in many other religions, the indwelling God in the hearts of man provides the basis for a personal relationship with Ultimate Reality.

4. Buddhism

Buddhism presents a special challenge to this study for the following three reasons: (1) Buddhism has no concept of a god; therefore, should one classify Buddhism as a religion or as a secular philosophy? (2) The void, for Buddhism, is considered <u>not</u> as something negative and alien; rather, it is embraced and made central to its understanding of reality. (3) Buddhism proposes to solve the problem of human suffering; yet, it denies the reality of the self altogether.

These paradoxical propositions regarding Buddhism must be examined because they directly impact the conclusions of the present study. They provide an alternative to how one is to understand and relate to the void.

First, is Buddhism a religion? For what it is worth, if one were to apply the criterion for tax-exempt status as a religious organization to Buddhism, it would not pass the Internal Revenue Bureau's "Supreme Being test." According to Theravada Buddhism, Gautama Siddhartha Shakyamuni, the historical Buddha and founder of Buddhism, neither claimed divinity for himself, nor appealed to any divine being to achieve Enlightenment. In fact, he expressly denied that he was divine; and he was agnostic as to whether or not there were divine beings.

Gautama's path to Enlightenment was a way, or method, to overcome suffering and achieve a state of eternal bliss. Nirvana could be attained without reference to a God or gods. According to Roshi Tjenshin Fletcher, "the very essence of his [Buddha's] teaching is that he was not a god, and that his realization is open to each one of us.[114] However, the problem is complicated by the fact that later Buddhist sects, e.g., Mahayana Buddhism, treated the Buddha with reverence approaching that of worship.

Buddhism is more than an atheistic, secular philosophy because it is a way of salvation, a total way of life—not only for the present, but for all eternity. Buddhism grew up in a Hindu culture and unconsciously assumed many of the presuppositions and cosmology of the Hindu religion, such as <u>dharma</u> (law), <u>samsara</u> (the cycle or rebirth), <u>karma</u> (the moral law of cause and effect), etc. Therefore, it can rightly be called a religion, albeit, a religion without a god.

The Buddha nature, or Buddha spirit, resides in all humans. Enlightenment is available for all human beings. That is accomplished by following the Four Noble Truths and the Eightfold Path. The Four Noble Truths are as follows:

1. Life is suffering.
2. There is a cause of suffering, which is desire.
3. There is an end to suffering.
4. Suffering can be overcome by following the Eightfold Path.

The first Noble Truth is that life is suffering (Sanskrit: <u>duhkha</u>). Humans suffer both physically and mentally, but the most profound suffering comes from misunderstanding the self. In Western thought, the self seeks individuation, self-actualization and fulfillment. However, in Buddhism, the goal is participation in and identification with the truly ultimate; therefore, from the Buddhist perspective, the aim of individuation is misdirected.

---

[114] Teshin Fletcher and David Scott, <u>Way of Zen</u>, p. 28 (New York: St. Martin's Press, Thomas Dunn Books, 2001).

The second Noble Truth is that there is a cause of suffering, which, according to the Buddha, is desire, i.e., attachment to notions or things. This only leads to disappointment and frustration, hence <u>duhka</u>, or suffering.

The third Noble Truth is that there is a path to overcome suffering and to achieve peace of mind.

The fourth Noble Truth is detailed in the Eightfold Path:

1. Right view or thought
2. Right intention
3. Right speech
4. Right action or discipline
5. Right livelihood
6. Right effort
7. Right mindfulness
8. Right concentration

If that were all that there was to it, then one might conclude that Buddhism was just another ethical lifestyle. However, in the foregoing Eightfold Path, the word "right" means to <u>be in accord with reality</u>, which leads to the next logical question: What is reality?

The term <u>Buddha</u> means to "be awakened"; but from what and to what? It means to become enlightened, i.e., to expose the illusions about oneself and life in general. According to Roshi Tenshin Fletcher in the <u>Way of Zen</u>, "In the absolute sense, Buddha is this vast emptiness, the unknown, that embraces our whole life without a moment of lapse, without anything missing."[115]

This leads to the second paradoxical proposition mentioned earlier regarding Buddhism. The void, or "vast emptiness of being," is called <u>Shunyata</u>. <u>Shunyata</u> is a key concept in Buddhist thought because at the heart of everything is <u>Shunyata</u>, or emptiness. There is no permanence

---

[115]   <u>Ibid.</u>, p. 47.

in the world. All is marked by transiency, contingency and impermanence. All is in flux and constantly changing. There is no essence to anything. People are born, grow to maturity; then age and die. Every situation, whether good or bad, inevitably comes to an end. The seasons change and with it the weather; mountains are formed and then they erode away. As a result, says Roshi Fletcher, "no moment of our lives is the same as the one before. So it is important to see that this is the nature of our life. When we accept it, we are at peace. If we don't, we are in trouble."[116]

If there is no permanence or essence to anything, then the Buddhist concludes that all is empty and without substance or meaning. What remains is emptiness, nothingness, the void. At the heart of the Buddha's realization is emptiness. When one enters the world of Buddhism, emptiness is not here or there, but everywhere. All is emptiness. When one realizes that, one ceases to chase after permanence and stability, after that which is fixed and unchanging.

Contemporary Buddhists go so far as to claim that modern physics supports their view of the universe. They say that physics shows that at the heart of all matter is emptiness and nothingness. There is no substance to matter.

> In quantum physics, ultimate reality is equated
> with formless energy (of physics) or shunyata . . .
> is not a state of mere nothingness, but is the very
> source of all life and the essence of all forms.[117]

The next step is this process of reasoning is to conclude that what is true of all else, is likewise, true of oneself; hence the doctrine of <u>annata</u>, or no-self. The self is only an illusion. It is only when one comes to terms with this truth

---

[116]   <u>Ibid</u>., p. 42.

[117]   <u>Ibid</u>., p. 35.

can one be freed from suffering. Once one has achieved that transcendent perspective on one's life, one is able to re-connect with all humanity and the universe. The self becomes one with ultimate reality and transcends individual concerns. This is a state of absolute peace and equanimity. The Japanese founder of Soto Zen, Eihei Dogen Zenji (1200-1253 CE) said, "To learn the way of Buddhism is to learn about oneself."[118] One not only is encompassed by emptiness (the void), one <u>is</u> the infinite void.

When a Westerner tries to comprehend Buddhist thought, the problem of terminology immediately surfaces. Terms do not mean the same in the two traditions. Just exactly what is meant by <u>Shunyata</u> (emptiness)? This study has determined that there are two basic ways that the term <u>void</u> is used: (1) as the <u>outer void</u>, or the absence of all matter, and (2) as the <u>inner void</u>, or the awareness of hollowness, lack, emptiness or meaninglessness in the human soul. For the purpose of analysis the two can be expressed as: Void I or Void II.

> Void I = the absolute vacuum, devoid of all matter.
> Void II = the loss of meaning and purpose

The question arises, how is the term <u>Shunyata</u> to be understood in Buddhism: as Void I, or Void II? It would appear that at times Void I is meant; and at other times, Void II. When pressed as to what is meant by <u>Shunyata</u>, the response seems to shift back and forth between the two as it becomes convenient. When Roshi Nagarjuna was asked if <u>Shunyata</u> meant Void I, the reply was, "This emptiness, or <u>Shunyata</u>, is the absence of an essence of things, but it does not mean their non-existence as phenomena."[119] Thus phenomena exists in <u>Shunyata</u> according to the Roshi.

---

[118] <u>Ibid</u>., p. 8.

[119] <u>Ibid</u>., p. 35.

At other times, when describing <u>Shunyata</u> it seems that the examples drawn from the physical world contradict that assertion. A text taken from the <u>Heart Sutra</u> (one of Buddhism's most sacred texts) reads:

> O Shariputra, all Dharmas are forms of
> emptiness, not born, not destroyed;
> Not stained, not pure, without loss, without gain;
> So <u>in emptiness, there is no form, no sensation,</u>
> <u>conception, deception, awareness;</u>
> No eye, ear, nose, tongue, body, mind;
> <u>No</u> color, sound, smell taste, touch,
> <u>phenomena</u> . . .[120] [emphasis added]

Therefore, according to the <u>Heart Sutra</u>, there is <u>no phenomena in Shunyata</u>.

At other times when asked to explain their understanding of <u>Shunyata</u>, they seem to retreat from rationality altogether and take refuge in intuitive experience. Nagarjuna stated that "It is false to say that things exist or that they do not exist. The reality lies in the middle, in <u>Shunyata</u>."[121] For the Westerner, things exist, or they do not; but what does it mean to be in the middle?

There is no doubt that Buddhism helps many people cope with the harshness of reality. Most would agree with the pragmatic argument that, "whatever works for you" is your truth, but the question arises for the Westerner: Is the Eastern way of thinking a viable alternative?

This study began with a description of the cartesian <u>Cogito</u>. It described how one's locus of certainty begins with the affirmation: "I think; therefore, I am." From that indubitable starting point, Descartes began to build out from that point to a larger understanding of the self and its world.

---

[120]   <u>Ibid</u>., p. 41 (emphasis added)
[121]   <u>Ibid</u>., p. 35.

However, the locus of certainty always remained with the existing individual. For Descartes, even the existence of God was the result of the rational ontological argument. The idea of God was an extension of human reasoning.

When the Westerner begins to assess Buddhist thought, the doctrine of <u>annata</u> immediately raises red flags. To begin by proposing to solve the human problem of suffering, and then to conclude that the self doesn't exist is tantamount to answering the question by getting rid of the questioner. How is that an answer? Is that not denying the reality of the question in the first place? The question is not solved but dissolved. That form of reasoning is like constructing arguments to convince a person that he or she does not have freedom, when that is an indisputable, direct and intuitive truth. Likewise, consciousness implies existence (I think; therefore, I am). One should be wary of any form of reasoning that does away with the reasoner.

The problem of <u>annata</u> becomes the great divide between Eastern and Western thought. The Westerner considers the self of central importance. The goal of life is to become fully individuated, self-actualized and fulfilled. Desire is not bad in and of itself. Indeed, it is natural and necessary for humans to aspire to ever greater accomplishments. That is their grandeur. It is when desire is used to seek improper goals at the expense of others that it becomes a problem.

The Easterner takes more of a passive approach to life. It is a lifestyle of acceptance of the "inevitable." One cannot fundamentally change anything about life. Indeed, life's goal is to escape the <u>samsara</u> of existence—to be released from the wheel of birth and rebirth.

Chapter XIII

SECULAR ANSWERS

This chapter begins an examination of several secular, i.e., non-religious, answers to the problem of the human predicament. In formulating a secular answer to the inner void, a major problem emerges: On what authority is an ethic grounded? Subjects of a tribe or nation might rebel against arbitrary laws promulgated by a king, emperor or dictator; consequently, those in power have resorted to divine sanction for their code of law. The Chinese philosopher Confucius recognized this problem and grounded his ethic on the "Mandate of Heaven." To act contrary to Heaven's Decree was to court disaster both to individuals and governments. The same justification was used by rulers like Hamurabi, Moses, Egyptian pharaohs, Greek kings, Roman emperors, Jesus, Mohammed and those in the European tradition who have proclaimed the Divine Right of Kings.

If a secular society rejects an authoritarian ethic for the norms of human conduct, then, it is left with the task of formulating an alternative answer with a more humanistic foundation.

1. Nihilism

One secular answer is that of nihilism. The Latin word <u>nihil</u> means "nothing". A nihilist, according to Webster, is one who holds that "traditional values and beliefs are unfounded and that existence is senseless and useless." Consequently, the nihilist believes in nothing. He rejects all social institutions and practices as to their claim of legitimacy and authority. Life is devoid of meaning and is absurd. The nihilist sees no hope in social causes and often becomes an anti-establishment protagonist, which leads to anarchism and terrorism.

Nihilism, as a political movement, existed for a brief period in nineteenth century Russia, but lost momentum because it was not self-sustaining. Once one has rallied around a cause—any cause—one asserts that certain values are worth fighting for, and perhaps dying for. Whenever one believes there to be something of value, something truthful like a universal ethic, then, one is no longer a pure nihilist. Thus nihilism, as a social or political movement, self-destructs.

Nihilism is more a philosophical mood than a movement. It is the philosophy that nothing matters. All is meaningless and absurd. It is a surrender to the absurdity of existence with no redeeming hope for the human situation. Nihilists have nothing constructive to offer humanity—only the counsel of despair. In response to the human problem, nihilism is mute. Consequently, secularists have sought elsewhere for a satisfying solution to an absurd world that exhibits no meaning.

2. Existential Humanism

An existentialist approach to life begins within the human situation and observes what can be learned without resorting to external ideologies that purport to define human reality in advance. It excludes all religious and philosophical systems that appeal to authority or divine revelation in order to interpret human reality. The existential approach seeks to know what can be discovered about human reality on its own.

As has been noted, the word "existence" comes from two Latin words meaning "to stand out from." Humans stand out from the rest of nature by their self-transcending freedom. Self-transcendence enables the individual to stand apart from its given situation, reflect on it, analyze it, and call it into question. Humans are not limited to what appears to be the case; they have the freedom to objectively review the situation in which they find themselves and change their course of action. That power is crucial to the concept of responsibility. Humans are held responsible for their actions. That is not true of the other animal species, who react according to stimulus and response.

Existential Humanism involves a commitment to the welfare of humanity; therefore, it needs an ethic that is comprehensive and universal enough to serve the needs of the human community. An ethic so relative as to be arbitrary would be ineffectual; likewise, an ethic that issued a set of absolute commands, such as in religious codes of behavior, would be counter-productive. What a secular humanism requires is an ethic that issues from within the human situation, and which would respect human freedom and diversity, yet would be binding upon the consciences of all. Lacking that universality, it would degenerate into something relative and without force so as to be virtually useless.

The Achilles heel of Existential Humanism has been its inability to muster traction for ethical behavior. It offered the option of ethical behavior as an intelligent rational choice; but, it could locate no foundation upon which to build a universal ethic. It is one thing to appeal to an individual to work for the common good of the community; but, it is another thing to insist that one has a binding obligation to do so.

The ethical universalism of Jeremy Bentham and John Stuart Mill argued for the view that one should always act in a manner that would bring the highest good to the greatest number of people. Unfortunately, that is not the way that most people decide their ethical behavior. They are more concerned with self-interest than the nebulous "common good." When push comes to shove, most people are unwilling to sacrifice short-term wants and needs for long-term social benefits, especially when those so-called "benefits" have no immediate reward for the individual and might even bring adverse effects.

A Secular Humanism that offered only the option of ethical behavior might appeal to an enlightened few; but still, it would be a choice and not a moral obligation. The existentialist philosopher Jean-Paul Sartre was so concerned to protect the freedom of the individual in ethical decisions that he undermined any basis for a communal ethic that would be binding upon all. He would allow nothing to bind the individual to freely choose its course of action. Personally, Sartre chose to live the ethical life; but, he stated that he might just as well have chosen its opposite. For Sartre, there was no transcendent moral law or authority that required the individual to live ethically. Thus Existential Humanism could offer no mandate for ethical behavior. If one opted not to live ethically, so be it!

An important truism for Sartre was the formula, "existence precedes essence," which meant that the individual freely chose its course of action—not the other way around. There was no prior essence that predetermined one's behavior. Each individual having chosen its course of action must take full responsibility for it. One cannot blame one's deeds upon any preconditioned nature or circumstance. That freedom is the unique dignity of the individual and is the grounds for holding the individual responsible for its actions. Each person is responsible for what he or she becomes in life.

Humans have the power to transcend the simple cause and effect relationship of nature, where every effect is predetermined by a cause. Without the freedom to stand apart from one's situation and be responsible, society could not exist. It would revert to the law of the jungle.

Existentialists may agree with the nihilist assessment that the universe exhibits no meaning or purpose and is absurd; but, the difference between them is in what to do about that absurdity. Does one simply surrender to the absurd, as the nihilist proposes; or, does one assert that humans can create their own meaning and values <u>in spite of</u> their absurd world?

Albert Camus, in his novel <u>The Plague</u>, described a physician, Dr. Rieux, who was a sophisticated, well-educated individual, but could find no religion or philosophy that met his needs. When an epidemic of the plague broke out in the city of Oran and thousands were dying on all sides, he was overwhelmed by the absurdity and wastefulness of nature in decimating lives and destroying so many homes. The offer of his limited services seemed like trying to sweep back the ocean with a broom; nevertheless, in spite of the absurdity of the situation, Dr. Rieux felt compelled to work tirelessly to save human lives. His commitment was to no higher power; it was to his fellow humans. He gave of himself without reservation or self-interest. In so doing, he typified the humanist credo of an unqualified commitment to humankind.

A military analogy of that humanist attitude would be: In the foxhole, it is not "Every man for himself and the devil take the hindmost"; it is the military code of honor where each man in the fighting unit can rely upon his buddies to go the ultimate limit to protect his life and safety. There is an unqualified loyalty to each other in the face of an absurd situation. That is the humanistic ideal. That is what raises humankind above the animal level.

3. Ethical Humanism, or the Ethic of Inquiry

Every human society has had a code of ethics to regulate behavior. An ethical code, whether written or unwritten, is necessary in order for a society to function properly. As has been noted, traditionally, the ethical imperative received its validation from religion. Divine sanction gave the code of behavior its ultimate legitimacy as reflecting the will of the gods.

From at least the time of the Babylonian king Hamurabi (c. 1750 BCE), rulers have sought to establish the authority of an ethical code by appealing to its divine origin. The black diorite steela, upon which is inscribed the Code of Hamurabi, depicts the king receiving the tablets of law from the sun god Shamash. This assertion of a divine origin buttressed the Code's claim to be the absolute and final authority for the Babylonian people.

The Hebrews, who were also Semites and emigrants from the Mesopotamian region, imported many laws from the Code of Hamurabi for their Mosaic Torah, e.g., the law of retribution, <u>lex talionis</u>, "an eye for an eye and a tooth for a tooth", etc. Moses is described as receiving the tablets of law from the Hebrew God, Yahweh, in much the same manner as Hamurabi did from Shamash.

A humanistic ethic avoids all such claims to divine origin of its code of behavior. It relies solely upon what can be derived out of the particulars of existence. An ethical maxim like the Golden Rule, for example, was chosen because it values the inherent worth and dignity of every person on earth—a key tenet for humanistic philosophy.

It has been stated that Secular Humanism needs to embrace an ethic that respects human freedom, yet is so universal as to be binding on the consciences of all persons. The question becomes: Is such an ethic conceivable, let alone possible? This study proposes that such an ethic is not only possible, it has been at work throughout human history from immemorial. It is based upon something so elemental and foundational that it is a part of every person's life on a daily basis. It is like the circulatory system that operates silently and unseen to preserve life whether one is consciously aware of it or not. It is something so obvious that ethicists have stumbled over it without noticing it; they have been "unable to see the forest for the trees".

The basis for this universal ethic lies in the way that the rational mind works, i.e., the dialectic of question-and-answer. This concept has been developed in the section on the Grandeur of Man and need not be repeated here. It suffices to say that the power to question reveals an ethical imperative built within it. Proving that, is the task of this present chapter.

This study shall endeavor to show that the power to question contains both an indicative and an imperative in its quest for truth. This fundamental operation of the mind becomes a bedrock starting point for a humanistic ethic because it is based upon something constitutive of what it means to be a human being. Without the power to question and act responsibly, humans would no longer be considered human; they would be indistinguishable from the rest of the animal kingdom. Humans, as has been noted, can be defined as the Inquiring Animal; and as a consequence of that, it is proposed that they also can be defined as the <u>ethical animal</u>.

For illustrative purposes, it is proposed that the topic be developed from a bit of dialogue taken from Shakespeare's <u>Hamlet</u>. Polonius imparts some fatherly advice to his son Laertes:

> This above all: to thine own self be true,
> And it must follow, as night the day,
> Thou canst not then be false to any man.[122]

If this sage bit of advice can be shown to be accurate, then truly, one has the possibility for a universal societal ethic based upon what it means to be "true to oneself." Such an experience presupposes that one knows that it means to be a

---

[122]   Shakespeare, <u>Hamlet</u>, Act I, Sc. iii, ln. 82-84.

self. One's access to selfhood is instinctive, immediate, direct and personal.

Socrates was fond of exhorting his fellow Athenians to "Know thyself", which presupposed that knowing oneself was the beginning of a virtuous life. For Socrates, the notion of self-knowledge was not just a private, introspective quest; it extended beyond the individual psyche to a cosmic consciousness, i.e., knowing who one is in relation to the order of the cosmos; which, for Socrates and Plato, meant the realm of Eternal Ideas or Forms.

Given the limited scope of this survey, one can offer only a broad outline of the steps necessary to describe how one moves from the concept of the self to a universal social ethic; nevertheless, given that proviso, the argument will be briefly stated.

This study began with the classical cartesian starting point in the Cogito (outlined in the Preface). Descartes found his certainty in the indubitable conclusion to his quest: "I think, therefore I am." It is out of an analysis of what it means to be a thinking being that one finds a clue to the ethical imperative lodged in one's very ability to think rationally.

That leads to the next step in understanding what is implied in being a questioner. In order to be a questioner, one must be a truth seeker. That is the indicative mode, since it is purely descriptive of the operation of the mind. A question seeks the true and correct answer to a problem. The answer must be responsive to what the question seeks. If one asks the elementary mathematical question: how much is two plus two? The answer is, of course, four—not three or five. Only the right answer will do. In mathematics, the formula $2+2=4$, is a tautology. By definition, the answer is known in advance.

When it comes to the interrogation of the natural world, one puts a question to Nature in the form of an experiment; and then, must await Nature's reply. The answer might be Yes or No, depending upon what is to be proved and how the experiment was designed. In short, the questioner seeks the true answer to its question and becomes a truth-seeker in the process.

In defining the self as a truth-seeker, one has located a decisive and crucial aspect of what it means to be a self. Over time, using the dialectic process of Q and A, each person becomes a <u>fund of truth</u> out of which the individual interprets itself and its world. Hence, truth constitutes the core of one's being—albeit, truth as one perceives it. As C. S. Pierce wrote, "Every man is fully satisfied that there is such a thing as truth, or he would not ask any question."[123]

This brings the inquiry to Polonius' first proposition, "to thine ownself be true." What does it mean to be <u>true</u> to oneself? Truth demands honesty and integrity; and to exhibit integrity toward oneself means to be at-one with the truth one possesses. The term "integrity" comes from the word <u>integer</u>, which is a "whole number". Integrity, therefore, connotes "to be whole", an undivided unity, to exhibit a oneness within one's being.

Self-deception, i.e., lying to oneself, is at the root of most psychopathologies. When one cannot face the truth about oneself and represses that truth in favor of a pseudo self-image, then one becomes a victim of mental disorders: neuroses, psychoses, phobias, fixations, obsessive-compulsive disorders, paranoia, schizophrenia, etc. When one loses touch with reality, i.e., the truth about oneself, then one begins to live in a fantasy world—the delusionary world of escapism and untruth. The psyche becomes divided, conflicted, subject to self-doubt, self-denigration, self-hatred, self-destructive behavior; and finally, disillusionment, defeat and despair. To quote Sir Walter Scott, "Oh, what a tangled web we weave when first we practice to deceive."[124]

The road leading back out of that psychological morass is a slow process of reclaiming one's integrity, i.e., getting

---

[123] C. S. Pierce, <u>Collected Papers</u>. Vol. V, par. 21 (1931-58).

[124] Sir Walter Scott, <u>Marmion</u>, VI, Introduction, St. 17.

in touch with one's inner self and seeking a self-affirmative, centered, focused, single-minded purpose and goal in life. One needs to restore self-respect, self-esteem, self-worth, personal pride and self-love.

Having said that, is one justified in taking the next step to the ethical life? Does it follow, as Polonius said, that "as night follows the day, thou canst not then be false to any man"? Can one say: ergo, a personal ethic translates into a social ethic? What are the logical connectors between a personal ethic (of integrity) and a social ethic wherein one is required to be truthful to others in a social context? Does being "true to oneself" mandate that one be open, honest and transparent to others? If being true to oneself means seeking what is in one's own best interest, then what happens when one's best interest and society's collide? The two are not always identical. Does one interest supercede the other? Should the individual's best interest be subsumed under that of society, or vice versa?

Before that knotty question can be resolved, one needs to establish more firmly the link between the individual and society. Most thinking persons would agree that it is in the individual's enlightened self-interest to participate in a just society.

One does not opt to join society as one would a club. One is already embedded in a social structure from birth; one is nourished and sheltered from harm by home and society. Long years of training and education have been invested in the youthful generation by the time that they reach adulthood. Unlike some animals equipped from birth to be self-sufficient, the human animal must undergo long years of care and protection before it can be self-reliant. Parents must watch over the maturation of their progeny from infancy to adulthood; and after that, society continues to provide services and protection throughout a person's lifetime.

It is for more reasons than convenience and security that society is necessary. According to Aristotle, "Man is by nature a social animal."[125] The individual finds his or her fulfillment in a life of social intercourse and mutual caring. The best interests of the individual lie in being part of the social matrix where one finds recognition, self-actualization, acceptance, love and personal validation. Therefore, to be "true to oneself" means to be true to the full range of what it means to be a social being.

Since a person is an integral part of society, for most, life apart from the social context would be unthinkable. It would mean the loss of all the values and benefits that living in a reciprocal social order brings. Life would indeed be dull, lonely and uninteresting without the social context. If one were to sever all ties with the social matrix, then life for most would be left without meaning or purpose.

Thus, the choice to become a hermit and to opt out of society entirely, for most persons, is not a real alternative. Social ties are too strong, extensive and rewarding even to contemplate such a choice. We need one another. People need community. Only in community are we fully human. Therefore, "being true to oneself" means being true to one's social nature.

This leads to the next level of social interaction, i.e., the ethical stage. At this juncture, the search for what it means to be a self moves from the indicative to the imperative mood. The indicative mood described how the human mind works, i.e., according to the question-and-answer dialectic; whereas, the imperative mood encounters another requirement—how the mind must operate within a community of inquiry. It involves the nature of truth-seeking, as such.

A self needs a fund of truth in order to function; but one soon learns that one needs more truth than one can discover on one's own. What is needed is a community of truth-seekers, because truth is a public venture.

---

[125]   Aristotle, Politics, Bk. I, Ch. 2.

When two or more truth-seekers collaborate, a community of inquiry is established. It is at this stage that an <u>ethic of inquiry</u> comes into play. A member of a community of inquiry is bound by a strict code of absolute truthfulness. In the sharing of truth, there is no room for duplicity or deception. One is required to be true to the truth that one possesses.

The model for a community of free inquiry would be the scientific community. Science is a public venture. The scientific method is a methodology that is open and available to all who seek truth in the empirical world. Science is self-regulating in that all new claims to truth are subjected to rigorous testing by independent laboratories. There is no room for fudging or falsifying the data in order to achieve the desired results. If any member of the scientific community attempts to perpetrate a fraud, they are immediately discredited and shunned by other scientists. As a community of inquiry, science is exemplary in its oversight and diligence in requiring every new truth-claim to be independently verified. Partnership in the truth-seeking venture requires, and will not tolerate anything but, total honesty and the duty to be truthful.

In science, truth is a public venture. It is a mutual activity; as one receives the truth, so one incurs the obligation to share that truth. A truth-bearer becomes a truth-sharer. Truth is a community property, not a private possession. Thus, as a truth-seeker and a member of a community of inquiry, one incurs moral and ethical obligations that reveal the true nature of selfhood.

Actually, there never was an isolated truth-seeker. One has always been a part of a community of inquiry because society, in the larger sense, is just that type of community. One can speak of the isolated, independent truth-seeker only for the purposes of analysis. Humans do not elect to join the community of inquiry; as has been noted, they are already enmeshed in it from birth. Each person finds his or her fulfillment in the reciprocal ethical relationship of being co-partners in the quest for truth.

It is often said that one cannot derive an "ought" from an "is"; that is to say, the imperative and the indicative deal with two radically different realms that do not intersect. The realms of fact and duty are like oil and water; they do not mix. However, it is clear that in this one instance, the integrity involved in the inquiry process requires that both indicative and imperative be part of the same mental event. In this one instance, both indicative and imperative do intersect.

The ethical imperative is grounded in the nature of truth-seeking as such. Truth-seeking is not an option; it is constitutive of what it means to be a human being. And "truth-sharing" becomes an obligation for everyone who participates in the human community. Thus the moral imperative comes from within and is a "stand alone" true requirement of the human psyche. Of course, just exactly how one fleshes out that ethical imperative is relative to a given culture. In that sense, every ethic is a situational ethic.

If it be true that the ethical imperative comes from within, and the evidence for this seems convincing, then, one can build an entire ethical superstructure on that rock-solid foundation. That means that an essential ethic is possible. It can be more than a recommendation. It is an imperative incumbent upon all humanity to heed. It is an obligation, not just an option.

As has been stated, all societies are based upon a code of ethics. To be a social animal, also means being a <u>moral animal</u>. As a member of society, one necessarily must affirm and embrace ethical behavior toward one's fellow citizens. Therefore, being "true to oneself" means being true to one's moral nature, which involves truthfulness to others. As Socrates taught, being true to oneself meant living the virtuous life. It means, not only to <u>know</u> the truth, but also, to <u>be</u> the truth—to live in harmony with the moral imperative within. Just as one is impelled by the drive for personal integrity as a truth-seeker, so it is mandatory that one live with the same integrity toward society. Therefore, it follows from being "true to oneself" that one "cannot live falsely toward any man." To do otherwise, would mean to be inauthentic and untrue to oneself.

What might an ethical system look like based upon this moral imperative? The most comprehensive social ethic is the familiar Golden Rule, which is found in many diverse cultures around the world: "Do unto others as you would have them do unto you."[126] Many Westerners believe that it originated with Jesus of Nazareth; but he was simply restating the Mosaic Torah: "Love your neighbor as yourself."[127]

Rabbi Hillel (1st century BCE) was once asked to give a summary of the Mosaic Law while standing on one foot. He offered a negative form of the Golden Rule: "What is hateful to you do not unto your fellow man. That is the whole law and the rest is commentary."[128] Other cultures around the world have similar maxims like the Golden Rule.

In the sixth century BCE over five hundred years before Jesus, the Chinese philosopher Confucius (551-479 BCE) offered the following statement in his Analects: "What you do not want done to yourself, do not do others."[129] The same ethical norm is found in Hindu scriptures, "Do naught to others which if done to thee would cause thee pain."[130] And again, in the Zoroastrian text Zend-Avesta, "That nature alone is good which shall not do unto another whatever is not good unto his own self."[131]

---

126   Luke 6:31.

127   Leviticus 19:18.

128   Pirke Avot (Ethics of the Fathers).

129   The Confucian Analects, Bk. 13, 15:20.

130   Ramayana, V, 1517, quoted in Indian Wisdom. p. 448, (London: Sir Monier-Williams, 1893.

131   Zend Avesta, Shayast-la-Shayast, xx, I, quoted in The Ethical Religion of Zoroaster, by Milasa Dawson (New York, 1931).

The Rule is also found in the Greek philosopher Diogenes Laertius: "We should behave to our friends as we would wish our friends to behave toward us;"[132] and again, in the advice of the Roman Emperor Julian (332-363 CE): "Act towards me as you think I should act towards you."[133] There is another form of the Rule stated by Mohammed in the Koran, "Wrong not, and ye shall not be wronged."[134]

The notion of a natural law implanted in the human conscience that is superior to any ethical maxim formulated by a particular religion is evident from the wide diversity and antiquity of the Golden Rule as reflected in the above sources. To quote the last will and testament of the skeptical priest Jean Meslier (1678-1733 CE):

> To discern the true principles of morality men have no need of theology, of revelation, or of gods; they need but common sense. They have only to look within themselves, to reflect upon their own nature, to consult their obvious interests, to understand that virtue is an advantage, and that vice is an injury, to the beings of their species.[135]

There were two things that filled the mind of the philosopher Immanuel Kant (1724-1804) with wonder and awe: "the starry heavens above me and the moral law within me."[136] That moral law within was expressed by Kant: "There is . . . only a single categorical imperative and it is this: Act

---

[132] Diogenes Laertius: Lives of Eminent Philosophers, v. 21.

[133] The Age of Faith, p. 17, Will Durant (New York: Simon and Schuster, 1950).

[134] The Al Bagarah Sura II:279b Qur'an.

[135] Quoted in The Age of Voltaire, p. 615, Will Durant (New York: Simon and Schuster, 1965).

[136] Immanuel Kant, Critique of Pure Reason, p.

only on the maxim through which you can at the same time will that it should become universal law."[137] That Kantian maxim is simply a philosopher's way of stating the familiar Golden Rule: "Do unto others as you would have them do unto you."

The ethical imperative embodied in the Golden Rule is not specifically religious in nature. It is a prudential maxim based upon what all persons instinctively know. Everyone knows how they want to be treated. It involves mutual respect. No one wants others to steal, lie, cheat, violate one's spouse, harm, or murder oneself. All those hostile behaviors are proscribed by the spirit of the Golden Rule. All ethical prohibitions and commandments, according to the Apostle Paul, are summed up in this saying, namely, "Love your neighbor as yourself;"[138] and "The law is fulfilled in one word even this: 'You shall love your neighbor as yourself.'"[139]

If one loved and respected the rights of a neighbor, then one would treat that neighbor with the same dignity and respect that one would wish for oneself.

Being a truth-seeker implies being truthful to others with no dissimulation, duplicity, deception, dishonesty or disingenuousness. Being phony, misleading, insincere, masking one's true intentions, lying, etc., all are antithetical to the truth. As the author of the first epistle of John in the Christian Bible wrote, "No lie is in the truth."[140] Any artificiality, falsehood or deceptive practice is in opposition to being true to oneself.

In summary, it has been shown that one can and must move from a personal ethic of integrity to a communal ethic without reference to an externally imposed authoritarian rulebook religion. The existential ethic outlined began with

---

[137] Kant, <u>The Metaphysic of Morals</u>, ch. 11.
[138] Romans 13:9.
[139] Galatians 5:14.
[140] I John 2:21.

the bedrock awareness of the existing self. From there, it was a matter of unpacking the logic implied in the dialectic of question-and-answer. Truth-seeking involves one in the integrity of the self, which requires that a person be at-one-with-the-truth in one's inner being. In order to be true to oneself, it must include one's social nature; and hence, one's moral nature.

A universal ethic is aptly summarized in the prudential maxim of the Golden Rule. Secular Humanism, therefore, has an inner-directed ethic. The void of Nihilism has been replaced by an affirmative, authentically human existence.

Ethical humanism offers a compassionate and just society. Such a society would treat everyone equally and fairly regardless of position or social status. It would respect the dignity of each person as a valued member of the human family. A just society is essential for harmony and order in the human community. Its requirements are summed up in the familiar maxim: Do unto others as you would have them do unto you." If everyone lived by that Rule, then there would be much less crime and need for law courts. It would be a compassionate society with a concern for the welfare of its members and a place where their civil rights were honored and respected. Honor and respect are basic requirements for any just society.

Without justice and fair treatment for all, people become angry and resentful. An unjust society produces conflict and chaos. It is the formula for disintegration of the social order, which in turn brings crime and confusion. A just society is an essential component of a happy and contented life. A person's innate sense of justice calls out for it as a basic requirement of the inner self.

What would a secular answer to the inner void be like? The next chapter on the Beautiful Life seeks to outline what would be involved in such a life. It is an attempt to flesh out what the Beautiful Life would be like lived in a secular context.

Chapter XIV

THE BEAUTIFUL LIFE

Socrates impressed his contemporaries as one who lived the Beautiful Life. In a prayer to the god Pan, Socrates said, "Give me beauty in the inward soul, and may the outward and inward man be at one."[141] Socrates was a person of integrity who lived at one with himself. He possessed a moral authority that came from deep within his soul; and was a living exemplar of all that he taught.

One of Socrates' key sayings was, "Knowledge is virtue." In other words, right knowledge leads to virtuous living. Life is not just a conglomeration of things. It is living out of <u>first principles</u>; and then, all else follows naturally. Socrates was a moral mentor, not only because he taught about the beautiful life, but because he lived it.

In modern parlance, the "Beautiful People" are those who are wealthy or famous, and whose lifestyle is usually expensive and well-publicized. They are the jet-setters who are always in the news. Socrates would disagree with that definition of the beautiful people. He criticized those who seemed to care about riches, or anything, more than virtue. It is the virtuous life that is the happy and fulfilled life. He said,

---

[141]   Plato, <u>Phaedrus</u>, sec. 279, Irwin, op. cit., p. 329.

> I do nothing but go about persuading you all, old and young alike, not to take thought for your persons or your properties but first and chiefly to care about the greatest improvement of the soul. I can tell you that virtue is not given by money, but that from virtue comes money and every other good of man, public as well as private.[142]

Four hundred years later, another moral teacher, Jesus of Nazareth, proclaimed a similar message, "Seek first the kingdom of God and his righteousness and all these things shall be added to you."[143]

This chapter on the Beautiful Life continues to derive the logical consequences that result from living out of first principals. In the chapter on the Grandeur of Man, it was determined that the human being was an <u>inquiring animal</u>. That finding became the basis of subsequent chapters for two important assertions about human beings—the human is: 1) a <u>truth-seeking animal</u>, and 2) an <u>ethical animal</u>. Arguments supporting those conclusions need not be repeated. It suffices to say that truth-seeking and ethical behavior were established as core values, both on the personal and interpersonal levels.

When choosing between alternatives, the inquirer necessarily exercises a value judgment. Therefore, a third consequence following from that notion is: the human is a <u>value creating animal</u>. When Socrates said that the unexamined life was not worth living, he meant that a life needs to be examined critically to see whether it is being lived for things of lasting value, such as: goodness, truth and justice. For Socrates, the beautiful life was one lived in harmony with those values; and if that be done, then one lives in harmony with oneself and others.

---

[142]   Plato, <u>Apology</u>, 38, Irwin, Ibid., p. 84.
[143]   Matthew 6:33.

Human life is value-laden. A value is something deemed worthy of one's commitment. It is a measure of worth and its cost is judged in terms of the time, effort and money expended to achieve that goal. A value is something prized so highly that it is worth striving for, and in some cases, dying for. Values that tend toward the creation of a holistic self-understanding are considered <u>core</u> values.

All values are ultimately human values, because humans are the one's doing the valuing. Humans assign worth to ideas, actions and possessions. That which is not valued is discarded as useless and without purpose.

On a personal level, values bring satisfaction, happiness and a sense of fulfillment. Values make life worth living, enrich existence and endow it with meaning. In answer to the question about what is necessary to fill the inner void, values are the answer. Deep down, they are what everyone seeks. When the inner soul is filled with good thoughts, good deeds, and good values, then one lives a wholesome and happy life. A value-filled life is a thing to be prized. It is a major asset and the key to happiness, bringing peace and harmony into one's life.

There is a whole spectrum of values that contribute to a holistic life. The full range of values would include all those previously mentioned in the section on Sizing the Inner Void: physical and mental health, psycho-social enrichment, intellectual, aesthetic, spiritual, ethical and volitional needs. All these values are necessary to make life satisfying and worthwhile.

On the community level, social values are those goals and principles deemed vital for the proper functioning of the body politic. Social values are those worthy of emulation by all members of a society. The question naturally arises: What values are needed by a humanistic society in order for it to function properly and survive? The values must be world-affirming, life-affirming and person-affirming. They also need to be non-authoritarian, existentially based, contextually appropriate and humanistically oriented.

Core social values hold a society together and provide its coherence. If its value system no longer coheres, the society comes apart and is destroyed from within. The people then are once more faced with social chaos and the meaninglessness void which awaits to swallow them.

The fourth consequence of being an inquirer is that the human being is a <u>self-evaluating animal</u>. The human not only places a value on everything that comes within its purview, it also has the reflexive ability to evaluate itself. That ability to pass judgment upon itself involves the capacity for self-transcendence. One's self-evaluation might be positive or negative depending upon the circumstances; nevertheless, such an evaluation is necessary if a person is to be a responsible being and be held to account for one's actions.

One's self-image is greatly dependent upon how one has been treated by others in the past—especially, during the formative years of childhood. However, that is not the only factor. One's self-esteem is affected by a variety of things, not the least of which is the discovery of one's own natural talents and abilities. Society also plays its role in providing a cultural image of humans in its metanarrative about the human drama.

A person's self-evaluation might be cast in the lowest terms, e.g., as a "dirt-bag", worthless and unworthy of esteem; or, in the highest terms as an exalted being, the creature in whom the universe comes into consciousness. One's self-understanding is constantly being influenced from without and within. There are always the ever-present external forces that would conspire to shape the individual's self-image; but, in the last analysis, it is the person's own inner evaluation that places a negative or positive value upon the self—whether it be as one worthless and of no value, or as one of priceless value and infinite worth. As Eleanor Roosevelt once said, "No one can make you feel inferior without your consent."[144]

The importance of self-interpretation becomes apparent in the fifth consequence of being an inquirer, i.e., the human is a <u>self-transforming animal</u>. The individual has the ability to shape its own character and destiny. There is no static essence which determines the course of human reality. As Jean-Paul Sartre has pointed out, each existing individual through active choices creates its character or essence. Man is not a predetermined entity; rather he is a work in progress. He or she shapes a personal character through freely made choices.

Socrates was known for his incessant questioning, especially with regard to moral issues. He never ceased to challenge his fellow Athenians to examine their opinions in order to see if they would hold up under critical scrutiny. Opinions are like noses—everyone has one; but opinions are not knowledge. Knowledge, according to Socrates, comes when one can give a rational defense of one's opinions.

Socrates often mentioned that his mother was a midwife, helping other women give birth to newborn babies. Socrates claimed that he too was a form of midwife, only he helped men give birth to their higher selves. His obstetric skill was in gently prodding others to perform the hard labor of delivering the truth. Socrates was keenly aware of the transforming power of the self. He was not interested in ideas or facts that did not pertain to moral self-improvement. For him, a person's first duty was to discover and promote moral development. His interest was primarily in ideas that could transform people's lives and make them better persons.

Perhaps, the most important source for self-transformation lies in the notion of what constitutes the <u>Ideal Human</u>. This Ideal has been associated with certain world historical figures such as Socrates, Jesus and Gandhi. They lived such morally superior lives that they became role models

---

[144] Anna Eleanor Roosevelt, <u>This Is My Story</u>, 1937.

for others. Their lives seemed to incorporate the ideal image of what life could be like when lived at its highest and best. Their moral authority came from within and was recognized by their contemporaries. People responded to those moral mentors because they saw in them a reflection of a larger self-image than was exhibited in their own personal lives.

However, the question arises, from whence came this larger self-image—the Ideal Self? The archetype of the Ideal Self seems to come out of the collective unconscious of the human race. The collective memory of humanity has stored within it the archetypal patterns of human existence. According to the Swiss psychoanalyst, Carl Jung, some major archetypes include birth, death, rebirth, power, magic, unity, the hero, the child of God, the demon, the old wise man, and the earth mother. One of those patterns conceivably would be a concept of the Ideal Human who would embody the highest and best in the moral history of humankind. It is a moral compass embedded in the heart of every person. It points the individual in the direction of the true spiritual north. That is the upside of this collective blueprint for moral behavior.

The downside is that the individual becomes keenly aware that it has fallen short of the Ideal Image. A comparison between the ideal and the actual brings an awareness of moral failure, causing guilt; hence, the notion of <u>fallenness</u>.

The sense of fallenness has been pervasive throughout human history. Hesiod, in his <u>Theogony</u> (c. 700 BCE), recounts the Greek concept of fallenness. According to Hesiod, human history was divided into four stages. The first was the Golden Age when humans lived in perfect harmony with nature and each other. In the succeeding Silver Age, people began to fall away from that Ideal. The trend not only continued, but increased during the Bronze Age until humankind degenerated to the level of the Iron Age where evil and lawlessness reached its zenith, which Hesoid identified with his own. (The Hebrew Bible gives an account of the declining Babylonian kingdoms of: Gold, silver, bronze, iron and clay.)[145]

The Hebrews told a similar tale about the fall of humankind, which began in a Garden of Paradise where humans and animals lived in idyllic harmony. But that time of bliss was shattered when the Primal Couple ate the forbidden fruit and began a downward spiral for the human race.

However, an existential interpretation of the Fall would characterize it, not as a historical event, but rather, as an interior event experienced in the lives of Everyman and Everywoman in all ages. What would the inner void represent, given this interpretation of fallenness? The sense of the void within would symbolize a state of alienation and estrangement from one's Ideal Self. Such an estrangement would not be from a transcendent divine Being; rather, it would represent the disparity between Possible Man and Actual Man. The alienation would be from one's Higher Self, one's True Self. Reconciliation would represent bridging that gap and filling the void with that which would make the self whole again. That is true authenticity.

In light of this discussion about the self-transforming powers of the human being, the next question that needs to be addressed is: what <u>transforming values</u> need to be emulated in order for the individual to live a full, happy and satisfying life; or, to put it in Socratic terms: What constitutes a beautiful life? The answer to that crucial question brings us full circle back to the original question of this study: What is needed to fill the inner void and make one whole? What do humans seek and require in order to live a happy and fulfilled life? Answering that is finding the holy grail of the soul's inner quest.

---

[145] See Daniel 2:31-45 in the Hebrew Bible, which gives a similar account of declining Babylonian kingdoms of: gold, silver, bronze, iron and clay.

What constitutes the Beautiful Life? In order to answer that daunting question, one must be able to identify what a beautiful life has in common with a beautiful face and beautiful music. It has been said that "beauty is in the eye of the beholder," suggesting that beauty is something relative—nothing more than a subjective emotion. But facial, tonal and spiritual beauty all share something in common. Beauty involves objective elements such as: symmetry, proportion, balance and harmony.[146] A beautiful life is one that is in balance and harmony with four key levels of existence: (1) oneself; (2) others; (3) one's Source; and (4) Nature.

First, living in harmony with <u>oneself</u> is directly related to one's self-evaluation. If one dislikes oneself, or perhaps, even hates oneself, then the inner self becomes divided against itself. The state of being conflicted within lies at the heart of most psychological disorders. When the self is at cross-purposes with itself, it contributes to psychic warfare between the survival instinct and the death wish (thanatos). That is inauthentic living.

The conflicted life is the opposite of living in harmony with oneself. In our former discussion on the value of integrity, it was pointed out that integrity involved adherence to one's code of values—chief of which was complete honesty and transparency of the self with itself. No duplicity or self-deception was permitted if one is to live a holistic life. Integrity involves a soundness of soul so that one lives out of one's center, i.e., out of one's strengths, rather than weaknesses.

When Socrates, in his prayer to the god Pan, asked that his "outward and inward man be at one," he was affirming

---

[146] The Greek philosopher Pythagoras was the first person to discover the mathematical basis for the notes on the musical scale. He measured the length of the strings needed to form each tone in the musical scale. Pythagoras proved that musical harmony had an objective mathematical basis.

the core value of integrity. Those who knew Socrates personally could sense that he lived in harmony with himself. Therefore, his friend Phaedo could say of him, "Of all the men of his time I have known, he was the wisest, the justest, and the best."[147] The value of recalling moral giants like Socrates is to remind ourselves of the life that can be ours; and for those who seek the Beautiful Life, knowing that is paramount.

The second key area is living in harmony with <u>others</u>. However, that is easier said than done. The twentieth century ethical scholar Reihold Niebuhr reminded us of "man's inhumanity to man." One cannot always control the behavior of others; especially, if someone has set out on a course of exploitation and you are the mark. One's response in terms of balancing love and justice is not always easy, but the principle rule of ethical conduct still is the familiar Golden Rule. It is based upon the premise that everyone instinctively and naturally knows how they would like to be treated by others.

The individual does not want others to deceive, prevaricate, steal, exploit, cheat, harm or demean them in any way. Consequently, when one treats others in a manner that respects their egos, property and civil rights, then one lays a foundation for fair and just dealings with one's fellow humans. A consistent demeanor based upon that equitable principle builds a reputation of fairness and respect for others that evokes a similar response from them. For Socrates, the virtuous life was one lived in harmony with truth, goodness and justice; that in turn leads to harmony with others.

If one were to ask what historical person said, "Do not return evil for evil," most people might respond that it was Jesus of Nazareth; but in reality, it was Socrates. Similar statements were made by Jesus, but not in those exact

---

147   Plato, <u>Phaedo</u>, Irwin, op. cit., p. 189.

words.[148] Those were the words and teaching of Socrates four centuries earlier. He taught and lived the Beautiful Life. As the psalmist wrote, "How good and pleasant it is when brothers live together in unity."[149]

The third area with which persons need to be in harmony is their Source, however that might be interpreted. Achieving oneness with Ultimate Reality is probably the most difficult of the four areas, because it involves knowing one's role in "the grand scheme of things." One does not adequately know oneself, however, until one knows oneself in relation to the Totality—that which is All-Encompassing.

To complicate things, the pattern of fallenness and the urge to reconnect gets repeated in relation to one's Source. The individual feels estranged from its Source, yet longs for reunion and participation in the fundamental Reality. Modern humans are aware that the universe operates according to natural law that is impersonal and indifferent to human aspiration. As conscious, rational and free beings, they are aware of standing apart from the mechanical forces of nature. There seems to be no way to bridge that dichotomy. The individual knows itself to be finite, contingent and transitory; but the universe, for all intents and purposes, is the opposite.

However, in spite of that intractable division, the individual is acutely aware that it is not an independent, self-generating entity. It is not the author and source of its own being. All life came out of the cosmic womb, including the human reality; therefore, humans are children of the universe. That was true in a literal sense in that even the molecules of the human body were formed under the extreme condition

---

[148] The Apostle Paul used the words, "Do not be overcome by evil, but overcome evil with good." (Romans 12:21); but then, Paul was familiar with Greek philosophy and he even quoted their poets (Acts 17:28).

[149] Psalm 133:1.

of a supernova explosion. As the astronomer Harlow Shapely once said, humans are made of "starstuff." The evolution of the universe included all life forms—of which humans were only one species among millions. One's Ultimate Source, in a secular context, would be the Cosmos; and, as the astronomer and science spokesman Carl Sagan often said, "The Cosmos is all that was, all that is, and all that ever will be."[150]

Therefore, on purely naturalistic grounds, the human race knows that life has evolved over billions of years through the process of natural selection. Having evolved to the level of conscious being, humankind can reflect upon its destiny and its place in the universe. Consequently, the human is in the strange position of belonging to, yet feeling separate from its source. This ambivalent situation leaves the human troubled and frustrated. It longs for reconnection and union with its Source, but is blocked in its attempt to fulfill that desire. No wonder the human being feels lost and an alien in its homeland.

The problem is endemic to the human situation. One belongs to, and originated out of, the Cosmos; but with the advent of consciousness, the human knows himself to be distinct from its cosmic origins. The ambivalence leaves the human being suspended, so to speak, in midair without a place on which to stand. An abyss has yawned open—an infinite abyss over which the individual is suspended. An urgent solution is required for the human predicament. The human being seeks closure on the perennial problem of estrangement at almost any cost.

Now, it becomes apparent why no finite value can answer the need of the inner void. The void within represents an insatiable hunger, a longing to reconnect with the Infinite, with one's Ultimate Source—the Cosmos. Therefore, the soul's inner quest for completion and fulfillment moves beyond personal and interpersonal realms to the

---

[150]   Carl Sagan, <u>The Cosmos</u>, p. 1.

transpersonal. It enters onto a new landscape of the soul where its horizons merge with the transcendent dimensions of existence.

Living in harmony with one's Source—the Cosmos—means several things. First, it means respecting its laws and cosmic order. One cannot reasonably defy the law of universal gravitation, as formulated by Sir Isaac Newton. For example, one cannot step off a cliff expecting to float like a bird on the air currents, i.e., without the use of human contraptions like parasails. If one does, the law of gravity will quickly decide one's fate. Knowing and obeying the laws of the universe is basic to living in harmony with one's Source.

Second, discovering and harnessing the forces of the universe is an important synergistic part of living in harmony with the Cosmos. Humankind's ability to harness the natural resources of fossil fuel, bio-mass, hydro-electric, wind, solar, geothermal, tidal and atomic energy are signs that humans are, at least on some points, living in harmony with the universe. By employing these manifold sources of energy, it becomes the responsibility of the human race to preserve and not destroy the ecosystem of our world.

Third, we must know our place in the universe, and for 21st century persons that means the Hubble universe with its virtually infinite cosmic expanse. It humbles us and makes us keenly aware of our finitude and temporality. We are only a tiny speck in the vastness of the Cosmos. The size and age of the Cosmos is mind-boggling. We stand in awe and wonder at its immensity and beauty. Consequently, the universe produces a deep sense of reverence and humility akin to that of a religious experience.

Since we are children of the universe, we need to learn what it has to teach us. Cosmologists and mathematicians tell us of its symmetry, beauty, elegance, order and unity—from the subatomic to its galactic levels. Although this is not a text on science, particle physicists point out that all known forces in the universe can be reduced to four fundamental forces in nature. Physicist James S. Trefil describes it as follows:

> There are four fundamental forces known in nature. The forces of gravity and electromagnetism are familiar in daily life. The other two forces operate at the subatomic level and are not immediately available to our senses. They are the strong force, responsible for binding the parts of a nucleus together, and the weak force, which governs radioactive decay . . . . The historical trend has been to see apparently different forces as nothing more than different aspects of <u>the same underlying mechanism</u>.[151] [emphasis added]

Newton's law of gravitation is a case in point. Prior to Newton, everyone thought that there were two separate gravitational forces at work in the universe, one that attracted objects to the earth, and a different one that propelled the moon and stars in their orbits. It was due to the genius of Newton that he was able to show how there was only one universal gravitational force that governed the motion of all physical bodies whether on earth or in the heavens. Newton therefore "unified" these two forces and produced a unified theory of gravitation.

In our time, scientists have been able to show how two of the four fundamental forces can be unified into one—electromagnetism and the weak atomic force have been reduced to what they call the electroweak force. The goal of scientists is to continue to search for the Grand Unified Theory (GUT) that will explain how all forces of nature can be understood in one simple formula. They feel that this is

---

[151]   James S. Trefil, <u>The Moment of Creation</u>. (New York: Charles Scribner's Sons, 1983), p. 85.

possible because of the underlying symmetry and beauty of how these forces operate on the subatomic level.

What can laymen learn from this ongoing quest? First, that the underlying make-up of the universe has a unity and symmetry that is found throughout the entire universe. This ability to unite affects all life—even human life. The philosopher and Catholic theologian Pierre Teilhard de Chardin has asserted that:

> If there were no internal propensity to unite, even at a prodigiously rudimentary level—indeed in the molecule itself—it would be physically impossible for love to appear higher up.[152]

If that be true, then the force to unite and to live harmoniously with others in this crowded world would be the stronger force that eventually would overcome those forces of divisiveness and alienation that have plagued the human race throughout its long history. Confidence that the stronger force to love and unite will prevail is one of the most important lessons that the Cosmos has to teach us.

The Cosmos is as magnificent as it is mysterious. As the Roman emperor and philosopher Marcus Aurelius wrote of the Cosmos, "All things come from you, have their being in you and return to you."[153]

Fourth and finally, one needs to be in harmony with <u>Nature</u>. By Nature, one refers to the entire ecosystem of the Blue Planet, our Earth. Living in harmony with Nature involves not only enjoying its many benefits; but also, being a good steward of its life-giving resources. Our planet is like a spaceship hurtling through the vast void of outer space. It is

---

[152] Pierre Teilhard de Chardin, <u>The Phenomenon of Man</u>, bk. IV, chs., sec. 2.

[153] Marcus Aurelius Antonius, <u>Meditations</u>, IV, 23.

our only life-support system and if we befoul the space vehicle upon which we depend, we destroy not only our chances of survival; we also jeopardize all that the human race has struggled to create through its long history. Global warming due to our carbon emissions is a case in point. The Green Revolution requires that one live in harmony with Nature—not exhausting its resources, but learning how to replenish them. Effective recycling and finding clean, renewable energy resources have become the main priorities of the twenty-first century.

Perhaps, the best way to reconnect with Nature and achieve participation in one's Source is to recognize and accept one's finitude and absolute dependence upon the Cosmos and to live with a sense of stewardship and harmony with its order.

Life lived to the fullest involves living in harmony with all four areas that have been discussed: oneself, others, one's Source and Nature. It means receiving the gift of life with gratitude and wonder. All of this adds up to the Beautiful Life.

Everyone is born to live the Beautiful Life. It is the Good Life—a life that is fulfilling and satisfying because it is attuned to the first principles of existence. It is living out of one's core values in a consistent and unified manner.

The Beautiful Life is living in harmony with oneself, others, one's Source and Nature; consequently, it is a life that is moral, creative and caring—one which contributes to the betterment of one's community and culture. It is living in a manner that is constructive, positive and loving. It is affirmative living because it says "Yes" to life and its promise of self-fulfillment and authenticity. It answers to one's inmost longings and needs; as such, it is a void-filling, complete existence that offers lasting satisfaction.

Living the Beautiful Life does not mean that one is free from troubles and sorrows; however, by retaining a positive attitude, one can overcome all negativity and obstacles, turning potential failure into lasting success. This makes life exciting and creative—one of harmony and peacemaking.

The Beautiful Life is available to all who genuinely seek self-understanding and authenticity. Socrates said it all in his prayer, "Give me beauty in the inward soul, and may my outward and inward man be at one."

CONCLUSION

Now that the dots have been connected, what sort of picture emerges? Is it familiar and attractive; something satisfying and hopeful? Or, is it alien and threatening; something gloomy and depressing? Is the appraisal positive or negative?

Has the study achieved its goal? Has it located the holy grail of the inner quest? The study set out to determine the breadth and depth of the void—both outer and inner—and what it takes to fill that void. Upon discovering the infinite chasm within the insatiable self, it became necessary to limit the study to those elements offering a sense of wholeness to the innermost self. A complete and fulfilled life is a happy life; it is harmonious with all dimensions of existence. Finding the key to a happy life is equivalent to locating the holy grail of the soul's inner quest.

How one evaluates the results of this study depends in large part on whether one agrees or disagrees with the guidelines set down at the beginning in the Preface. There the universal problem of the void—both outer and inner—was defined as to: (1) scope, (2) presupposition, (3) methodology, and (4) goals. Any fair evaluation of the study should be cast in terms of whether the inquiry has adhered faithfully to its own guidelines and not that of some alien ideology.

> In measuring the scope of the investigation,
> it soon became apparent that its breadth was
> incredibly wide involving almost all areas of the

sciences and humanities. A limited, narrowly
defined problem of the self quickly became an
inquiry virtually without limits ranging over
the entire intellectual map. It spilled over into
the fields of psychology, philosophy, the arts,
literature, mythology, religion, astrophysics,
quantum physics, biology, geology, etc. Hardly
a field of thought was exempt from the reach of
the void—both outer and inner.

The problem is that the subject is so vast and all-
encompassing that one is hard pressed to know what is crucial
or irrelevant. Spatially, the void is larger than the cosmos and
smaller than a quark. Temporarily, history is bounded before
and behind by the eternal emptiness of the void. Physically, it
is found in outer space; and existentially, in inner space.

It is incumbent on the inquirer to clearly state the
problem of the void—both outer and inner. The outer void
was defined as nothingness; therefore, the problem became:
how does one discuss nothing? Perhaps, nothing can be said
about nothing; but something can be said about the human
experience of nothingness, a.k.a., the void.

As to the presuppositions of the inquiry, they were set
forth as accepting the reality of the self and its world. The
self was established as a conscious, self-aware being that was
the primary locus of certitude. That basic starting point was
arrived at through the cartesian <u>Cognito</u>. The only thing that
could not be doubted was the thinking, willing, feeling self.
That became one's primary certitude. From that, one could
build out to a rational understanding of both the self and its
world.

The world was not an Idealistic projection of the self;
rather, it was the phenomenal context in which the self came
into actualization in the fullest sense of the word. The world
presupposed was that of modern cosmology, i.e., the infinite,

expanding universe, which is the Source of all life and matter. Consequently, humans are children of the universe.

The universe comprises a vast expanse about which humans know very little. Human history is but a tiny point on an infinite time line that gives no clue as to its meaning or purpose. Thus, if human reality is to have any meaning or purpose, it must come from within. Humans are the source of their own values and goals. All claims to outside revealed truth were considered special pleading designed for the purpose of giving ultimacy and finality to one's ethical code. That left the human being alone and on its own to forge the values and ethics needed for survival in a communal context. This new autonomy requires boldness and a spirit of adventure. Humans are responsible for shaping their own destiny.

Beginning with those suppositions and proceeding with the phenomenological method as outlined by Edmund Husserl and Jean-Paul Sartre, the inquiry began to explore the void within and what it takes to fill that void, providing a happy and holistic existence. It offered a lifestyle of wholeness; hence, the subtitle of this study: "An Inner Quest for Wholeness."

Without reference to alien ideologies or claims of revelation from some divine source, the inquiry built step-by-step what could be known from an existential analysis of the human reality. It sought what was entailed in the concept of authentic existence from an existential perspective.

In response to the void within, several strategies were employed by humans to fill the inner void. The study examined: finite answers, religious answers and secular answers. Among the finite answers were: the lure of hedonism, wealth, fame, power, knowledge and philanthropy (to mention only a few escapist strategies). In the last analysis, they all proved empty and hollow leaving the individual without lasting deposits of satisfaction in the soul.

The wide spectrum of religious answers discussed—both past and present—all claimed to provide an infinite answer for the infinite void within. Undeniably, that has been a satisfying answer for many; although, even there, the great mystics have experienced what has been called, the "dark night of the soul" or "the absence of God" where all comfort and peace formerly experienced faded and became a lost and fleeting thing, leaving the seeker empty.

There are those for whom the religious answer no longer works; and for them, this study examined several secular answers to find out if there were viable alternatives. A secular humanist position was developed beginning with the self's power of discursive reasoning, which used the dialectic of question-and-answer. The study proceeded to elucidate the self-transcending freedom, integrity, truth-seeking, truth-sharing, value-creating, self-evaluating and self-transforming powers of the human being; and finally, the inborn ethical imperative that calls for integrity toward oneself and others. All of this led to a life lived in harmony with all dimensions of the self; and thus, to an understanding of authentic existence, or the Beautiful Life. Living the Beautiful Life means not fleeing from the Void; but facing it and filling it with meaning.

Michelangelo once was asked how he produced such magnificent sculptures like his David, Moses and the Pieta—perfect in every detail. He replied, "It is simple. You just take a block of marble and remove the unwanted material. What is left is what was there all along."

As every creative person knows, whether sculptor, painter, poet or writer, any great work of art begins with an idea or image of what one hopes to create; then, chip-by-chip, stroke-by-stroke, line-by-line, one discards that which is irrelevant and trivial, leaving the perfect expression of what one had envisioned beforehand. That ideal is hoped and striven for, but seldom achieved, except by the great artistic masters. The average artist struggles to create, but matter stubbornly resists.

Writing a book is much like sculpting. One begins with assembling a massive amount of research and independent, creative thinking; then, through the painstaking process of selection—accepting some and rejecting others—one gradually shapes an image that hopefully, reflects reality.

In describing the Beautiful Life, has this study included too much that was extraneous and unnecessary; or, has it eliminated too much, leaving only the bare bones of that life characterized by authenticity? Whether the book should be one-half its size, or several volumes in length is a matter of judgement. What the author has striven for is to establish the essential points that portray the possibility for a truly human existence derived solely from an existential analysis of the human condition. If it has accomplished that task, then, it has succeeded.

In conclusion, humans are defined by the void—not just in the sense of the outer physical void; but also, in the sense of the inner spiritual void. Human life is molded and shaped by this ever-present force, not just in a passive way, but by one's active response to the void. Just who and what one becomes, in large part, is determined by how one responds to the challenge of the mysterious, ubiquitous void that confronts every human with both a threat and a promise.

The threat is the eventual annihilation of all structures of meaning that one attempts to build. Ultimately, the void will engulf all human aspirations and accomplishments, both individually and collectively.

However, in spite of that bleak prospect, the void also encounters humans as a promise. By underscoring one's finitude and temporality. It calls out the highest and most noble hopes and dreams. It offers the possibility of a truly authentic existence.

The realistic choice in face of the vast and impersonal universe is not nihilism, the philosophy that nothing matters. The universe produced human life and endowed it with self-transcending freedom. It enabled humans to choose how they will respond to the promise of a fully authentic existence.

In the last analysis, that is the only valid alternative in light of what it means to be "true to oneself." Integrity demands that one choose the ethical and virtuous life which is an existence in harmony with all dimensions of life: oneself, others, one's Source and Nature. If one has achieved that, then one has begun to live the Beautiful Life.

It is said that when James Watson and Francis Crick discovered the double helix of the DNA molecule, they walked into the Eagle Pub in London and announced: "<u>We have found the secret of life!</u>" For that discovery, they received the Nobel Prize.

Likewise, it can be said of those who have learned to live the Beautiful Life, truly, they have found the secret of life. They have located the holy grail of the soul's inner quest. For true pilgrims of the soul, there can be no greater prize.

Printed in the United States
By Bookmasters